BE THE
SPARK

FIVE PLATINUM
SERVICE PRINCIPLES

for Creating Customers for Life

SIMON T. BAILEY

Simon T. Bailey International, Inc.
13506 Summerport Village Parkway, Suite 324
Windermere, FL 34786
888-592-1820
hello@simontbailey.com

Printed in the United States of America
ISBN-13: 978-1-7325994-0-6
ISBN-11: 978-1-7325994

CREDITS:

Collaborators:	Ellena Balkcom, Written on Purpose, Savannah, GA
	DL Barrett, Word Paper Scissors, Mt. Juliet, TN
Copy Editor:	Kathleen Green, Positively Proofed, Plano, TX
Design:	Kendra Cagle, 5 Lakes Design, Wolcott, NY

TABLE OF CONTENTS

FOREWORD

In 1950, a young man from Oklahoma opened a five-and-dime in Bentonville, Arkansas. Armed with nothing but a pickup truck and a big idea, Sam Walton signed a 99-year lease on his storefront in the town square, confident he would fulfill his burning dream: to bring discount retail stores to rural America, and "give ordinary folk the chance to buy the same things as rich people." By 1960, he owned 15 stores, and in 1962, he opened his first Wal-Mart, which would eventually become the third-largest retailer in the country. In 1985, *Forbes* magazine declared him the richest man in the world.

Despite this fame and success, Walton retained the same small-town modesty he was born with; in fact, he drove his 1979 Ford pick-up truck every day until his death, saying, "What am I supposed to haul my dogs around in, a Rolls-Royce?"

Walton's humble attitude showed itself most apparently in the way he treated people. He considered his employees as partners, sharing profits as well as constant words of praise and motivation, and he believed that boosting his employees' self-esteem was the key to accomplishing goals. Beyond his personnel, Walton knew the customer was king, and pleasing his customers became the driving force for all his business practices. The secret to success, he believed, is to "exceed your customer's expectations. If you do, they'll come back over and over. Give them what they want—and a little more." Although he didn't know it, Sam Walton was providing a SPARK for his company and his customers—a **SPARK** that would change the face of American retail.

In the future, you or your business will be paid for the moments you create, and for the differences you make in the customer experience. Today's successful leaders and companies, such as Amazon, Disney, Ritz-Carlton, Tesla, and American Express, recognize that simply meeting demands and sticking to a tried-and-true formula won't differentiate your company from the rest. Walton recognized this, saying, "There is only one boss—the customer. And he can fire everybody in the company from the chairman on down, simply by spending his money somewhere else." What Walton knew even then still holds true—today's customers are educated, prepared, and have more options than ever before. They are also more demanding. Turning customers into fans who are not only loyal, but also refer others, requires delivering exceptional customer service that exceeds expectations—every time.

You, your company, and your people must be the **SPARK** that brands each moment and creates the lasting impression. We call this extraordinary level of service commitment and experience Platinum

Service. You might be familiar with the Golden Rule—"Treat others the way you want to be treated." With Platinum Service, we take this one step further and abide by the Platinum Rule, coined by my good friend, Dr. Tony Alessandra: "Treat others the way **they** want to be treated." Just like Sam Walton knew all the way back in the 1950s, focusing on customer needs—and going above and beyond to meet those needs—should be the driving force that guides your actions. *Good* service is enjoyable; *Platinum Service* is **valuable** and **memorable**. It requires you and everyone in your business to take the time and make the effort to create signature moments that set you apart from the rest.

The purpose of this book—as well as the online course that offers a deeper dive into applying the **SPARK** concepts and tools—is to equip you, your team, and your business with a simple **SPARK** Framework so you can infuse your culture with a mindset to win—and keep—customers for life.

In every country, **SPARK** will look different based on local cultures and to what extent customer service is viewed as a differentiator. For example, recovery or response time expectations, greeting rituals, and other interpersonal nuances will impact **SPARK** interpretations. We are sensitive to and always advise our clients and partners to adapt **SPARK** and its concepts as best you see fit based on your region and/or target market.

INTRODU

CTION

When I started in the hospitality industry thirty years ago in Atlanta, Georgia, it was totally by accident. I got a job making $5.10 an hour and served as the front desk clerk, PBX operator, bellman, reservation clerk, and houseman at the Days Inn Downtown Atlanta. I didn't care that I was doing multiple jobs, because it kept my mind occupied.

I fell in love with the hospitality tourism industry. It got in my blood, and I decided to see if I could make a career of it. When some industry colleagues invited me to the monthly chapter meeting of the HSMAI (Hospitality Sales and Marketing Association International), I was all in. I met Ed Staros there, the managing director of the luxurious Ritz-Carlton Buckhead—the flagship for the fledging Ritz-Carlton Hotel Company that would soon redefine what it meant to be a global luxury brand.

Ed introduced himself, gave me his card, and asked me to call him. Later that night, as I took public transportation back to my drug-infested neighborhood, I wondered what—if anything—would come from my conversation with Mr. Staros.

The next day I got up super early to get to work. I worked the shift from 7:00 a.m. to 3:00 p.m., so all my days started early. I called Mr. Staros during my lunch break, and the operator transferred me to the executive offices. The lump in my throat was so big I could barely swallow. I was thinking, "Was I good enough to work at such a prestigious company?" I had made it past the gatekeeper; now what?

"May I have your name, please?" asked his secretary.

"Yes, I'm Simon Bailey."

"Thank you, Mr. Bailey. And what is the purpose of your call?"

"Mr. Staros gave me his card last night and asked me to call him," I answered.

"Thank you," she responded.

"Will you please hold?"

I expected to wait for several minutes and was surprised when she was back on the line in a few seconds.

> "Simon, Mr. Staros would like to schedule
> a meeting with you. Are you available
> next week?"
> she asked.
>
> "Um, sure. Of course!"

I answered, not knowing why a man in his position would want to meet with me, the clerk at a Days Inn. A meeting was set for the following Wednesday, just like that. What I didn't know is that in only ten days, my mindset on serving others—and my life as I knew it—would be dramatically shifting.

The day of the meeting finally came. I had requested a personal day off from the Days Inn and caught MARTA to North Atlanta, the posh section of town. I walked into the Ritz-Carlton Buckhead, and from the moment I stepped inside the doors, I was in awe. It was the most beautiful place I had ever seen. I was just a 19-year-old guy from Buffalo, New York, the third poorest city in America at the time. Until that moment, the nicest places I'd ever been included eating at Ponderosa and staying at the Holiday Inn on family trips.

I was wearing my Sunday best and looked casket sharp. Right away, I noticed the uniforms of the bellhops and the rest of the staff. They walked with a purpose and obvious pride. They smiled genuinely as they said...

> "Good morning, Sir."

The aroma in the lobby just smelled of class and over-refinement. The more I looked around, the more the hotel reminded me of something from a television show or travel channel.

I didn't know that anything like this actually existed in real life.

I approached the front desk and, to my surprise, was treated with respect. I asked to see Ed Staros.

He showed up in what appeared to be a custom-made Italian suit like I'd only seen advertised in fashion magazines. He wore crisp, white, starched shorts, the perfect tie, and polished shoes that were so shiny that light bounced off them. He had a powerful presence about him and, in an instant, I knew this guy was different. With evident pride, he told me about the hotel, how it was a flagship property and how anyone of significance would come through the Buckhead area of Atlanta. He then skillfully transitioned to the point of our meeting.

> "I want to offer you a job as a night manager here at the Ritz-Carlton Buckhead,"
> he said.
>
> "Your salary will be $22,000, and you will also receive benefits. Our motto is 'We are ladies and gentlemen, serving ladies and gentlemen.' You would be a perfect fit for our culture."
>
> I looked at him in disbelief.
>
> "Uh, thank you,"
> I said.
>
> "I need to think about this. Um, I'll call you and let you know."

I thanked him again and quickly exited the hotel.

On my way home, a thousand thoughts flooded my mind. Why did he want me to work there? What did he see in me? I didn't believe I had what it took to work at the Ritz-Carlton. As I reflect back on that moment, I am reminded that it's not who you are that holds you back; it's who you think you're not. Here I was, a front desk clerk making $5.10 an hour and the Ritz-Carlton Buckhead just offered me a job making $22,000 per year. WOW! Common sense would say take the job, right?

I called Mr. Staros the next day and told him thanks, but no thanks. Then I went back to the Days Inn and told my boss that I'd just turned down a job at the Ritz-Carlton. He stared at me, mouth agape. His eyes said it all: "You fool! Why in the world didn't you take the job? It's the most prestigious hotel in the city!"

PLATINUM SERVICE:
PUTTIN' ON THE RITZ

A few days later, I received a note from Ed Staros, handwritten on exquisite personalized stationery. He thanked me for coming to see him, and he encouraged me to stay in touch in case I changed my mind. As I think back, this encounter with Ed Staros and the Ritz-Carlton was my first experience with Platinum Service. Here was a place whose leader, brand, and motto were all about exceeding guest expectations and building strong relationships. My **SPARK** mindset was born, and like Sam Walton, I just didn't know it yet.

My encounter with Ed Staros and the Ritz-Carlton was my first experience with

PLATINUM SERVICE ...
MY SPARK MINDSET was born.

I never forgot that experience and the decision that shifted both my life and my career. I reconnected with Ed a few years ago when I ran into him at an industry event. He's now the vice president and managing director of both the Ritz-Carlton and the Ritz-Carlton Golf Resort in Naples, Florida. I mentioned our encounter thirty years ago. He remembered it well and said he still couldn't believe that I turned down the job. We both had a chuckle.

Even though I didn't take the job with Ritz-Carlton, I'd learned what "putting on the Ritz" looked like, just from that brief encounter with a few of the ladies and gentlemen whom I'd interacted with that memorable day. It was about treating everyone, regardless of background and age, with respect. It was about taking the time to create memorable service moments. It was about ensuring exceptionally great service at each and every interaction. Those principles became my standard for Platinum Service.

Several years later ... I was given an opportunity to work with my mentor, Cindy Novotny. She was a global trainer for Disney and founder of the internationally renowned training and consulting firm, Master Connection Associates (MCA). MCA was the exclusive, contracted training company for The Ritz-Carlton Hotel Company that also founded and wholly operated The Ritz-Carlton Leadership Center on their behalf.

Working with MCA as a consultant, I crossed paths with Ritz-Carlton again as I was given the opportunity to teach Ritz-Carlton Learning Institute content to their teams in Bangkok, Thailand, and Thibodaux, Louisiana. This time, instead of Ritz-Carlton being "the one that got away," I became part of the Ritz-Carlton team. In teaching their content, I was lucky enough to form a long-term relationship with this reputable brand that would forever impact my career.

My first experience with Ritz-Carlton as a young man showed me how to conduct myself in future customer and employer relationships. For example, I learned how important it is to look people in the eye, smile, and use their name early and often.

As symbolic as my experience was with Ritz-Carlton, my next opportunity to work in the hospitality industry would exceed my wildest imagination.

Ten years later... after two years of interviewing with the casting manager at Walt Disney World Resort, I was finally hired as a senior sales manager for park & events for the Walt Disney World Resort in Lake Buena Vista, Florida. I was elated to be working for one of the most renowned brands in the world.

Once new-hire orientation was complete, new cast members received an invitation to have breakfast with the president of Walt Disney World Resort. We were to arrive at Disney's Yacht and Beach Club resorts, a property near Epcot, at 7:30 a.m. the day after our orientation. Being the eager beaver that I had become, I decided to arrive at 6:45 a.m.

When I was escorted to our reserved table, I noticed the tables had name cards that indicated where we were to sit. I also noticed that my name wasn't next to the president. I confess I did something a little sneaky. Since there was no one in the room, I switched the name cards around so I could sit next to the most powerful man in the theme park division of the Walt Disney Company: Al Weiss, then president of the Walt Disney World Resort.

After we were seated, and Al had walked around and introduced himself to everyone, Al and I exchanged pleasantries and I said,

> "Al, may I ask you a question?"

> "Of course,"
> he answered.

> "What do I have to do to get ahead at Disney?"
> I boldly asked.

> Without missing a beat, he replied,
> "You need to know who you are,
> and why you are here."

I stared at him with a blank look on my face, as if to say, "Dude, is that it? Really?" I gave him my screensaver face and turned back to my meal. I didn't realize the importance of what he was *really* saying until years later.

You see, Disney didn't hire me to do a job. They hired me to create a moment; to create a **SPARK** that would ignite positive memories in the hearts and minds of the guests. During orientation, Disney captured my heart by telling the story of Walt Disney and why he built a theme park in Florida. To this day, I believe that Disney Casting intentionally took two years to offer me the job to be sure that I had the right mindset—that I was willing to go above and beyond to create memorable guest experiences each and every time. Once I understood this, it literally changed my life.

You see, Disney didn't
hire me to do a job.
They hired me to
CREATE A MOMENT.
Once I understood the why behind
what Disney really intended me
to do, it **literally changed my life.**

Sam Walton once said, "The way management treats the associates is exactly how the associates will treat the customer." Like Walton and other service forerunners, Disney was a company that understood how to engage employees. By treating their people with genuine care, Disney leaders generate a sense of pride and ownership in caring for the guests. As an employee, I felt part of a higher purpose—something truly special—as I performed my role in delivering exceptional customer service.

This is where my SPARK mindset—the principles of Platinum Service—was sealed. Platinum Service is about creating a culture that captures the hearts and minds of employees so they will, in turn, capture the hearts and minds of customers. This entails focusing on customer needs and knowing what actions to take to provide enjoyable and valuable service. Platinum Service means taking the time and making the effort to create branded, memorable moments that set you apart from everyone else! It means creating a **SPARK** of appreciation that catches fire in your culture and engenders distinguished and unforgettable—PLATINUM—Service.

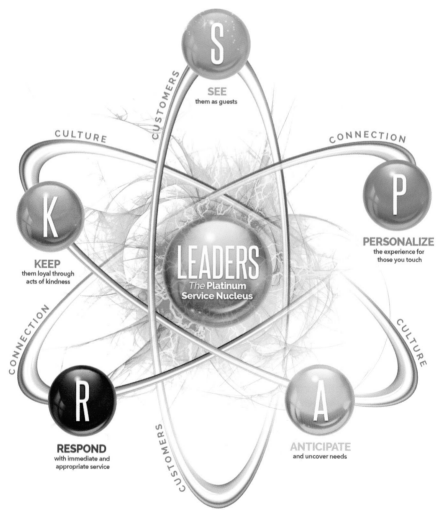

So, what will be the **SPARK** for you? Maybe you've had a Ritz-Carlton or Disney experience that changed the way you think about customer service. Maybe you're still searching for that brilliant moment. Either way, you have the opportunity to **Be the SPARK** for *your* customers, and this book will teach you how. **SPARK** invites you to use five proven methods to create moments that make a permanent impression in the minds and hearts of your customers, and to turn them into customers for life:

 SEE them as guests

 PERSONALIZE the experience for those you touch

 ANTICIPATE and uncover needs

 RESPOND with immediate and appropriate service

 KEEP them loyal through acts of kindness

As I've learned along my journey and through leaders such as Sam Walton, Ed Staros, and Al Weiss, **SPARK** isn't something you just do, it's who you are at the core of your being. As Al Weiss advised me, it's who you are and why you're here. Creating the **SPARK** for customer interactions means surpassing all expectations. It invites you to stop being mechanical and stiff when it comes to giving service and beckons you to understand and adapt to the emotions of those you serve. This is a mindset, a way of being.

In each of the following chapters, I share stories and examples that will **SPARK** a chord in you. I will give you tools, tips, and things to think about that will help you shift to a Platinum Service mindset. I also share evidence-based research that supports this approach. Each section concludes with recommendations or exercises on what you can do next. Also included is insight into how to implement the key concepts in your daily undertaking to make a difference for your employees, which will ultimately make a difference for your customers and your business.

Be the SPARK: Five Platinum Service Principles for Creating Customers for Life will teach you how to retain customers in a growing global market, turn customers into loyal fans, and create unforgettable moments that keep them coming back. In the words of the illustrious Maya Angelou, "I've learned that people will forget what you said, people will forget what you did, but people will never forget how you made them feel."

In a world of information and interaction overload, **SPARK** ignites an emotional experience that will make you unforgettable to your customers. Your interactions will become emblazoned in the souls of your customers, and they will remember them—and you—for life. Consider, for example, one of the biggest tech companies in the world: Netflix. Beginning in 1997 as a DVD rental service, and evolving into the largest streaming service in the world, Netflix revolutionized the way more than 100 million people worldwide watch TV and movies.

Netflix provides a **SPARK** for its customers by giving them a platform that is efficient, cost-effective, and personal. It uses an algorithm that recommends shows and movies based on personal preferences, and even offers the option to create separate profiles (and separate algorithms) for different members of the family—cartoons for the kids, romantic comedies for mom, action movies for dad—and they do it all for $10 to $15 a month.

Netflix uses its high-tech capabilities to create a high-touch relationship with the customers and effectively keeps its members for longer than any other streaming service. In 2016, only 9 percent of users canceled their Netflix service. Interactions—even virtual ones—make all the difference in delivering Platinum Service.

While Netflix is a modern example, its practices follow a time-tested truth: Exceptional service is unforgettable.

● ● ●

To take us back to where my Platinum Service mindset began, I remember staying at the Ritz-Carlton Atlanta hotel a while back. Leaving the hotel for a meeting, I realized I'd left my USB headset at home, and I needed it for a conference call I'd planned to take from my room later in the day. I called the Ritz-Carlton and asked for the concierge desk. A gentleman answered the phone, and I asked him if there was an electronics store close by. He told me there was a Best Buy ten minutes away from the hotel.

I decided that when my meeting was over, I'd go back downtown, stop in Best Buy, and then head back to my hotel for my 2:00 p.m. call. As fate would have it, my meeting ran over. I was racing back downtown to get to Best Buy when my cell phone rang. It was the concierge from the Ritz-Carlton.

"Mr. Bailey,"

he said,

"I want you to know that we went to Best Buy and picked up the USB headset for you. The charge has been added to your bill."

When I got back to the hotel, I wanted to leap across the desk and give him a chest bump like football players do. But since the ambience of the Ritz-Carlton is elegant, and ultra-conservative, I simply said,

"Thank you"

as I didn't think a chest bump was the right "gentlemen-serving-gentlemen option."

I learned some valuable lessons from these two front-runners in the Platinum Service game. The Ritz-Carlton Atlanta had succeeded in making me feel important and appreciated. Disney shifted my perspective from customer service is a department to Platinum Service is a mindset. And so, my **SPARK** story begins.

"

"Mayo Clinic is created
every day by every employee
in every interaction with
every patient."

— William J. Mayo, MD

CHAPTER

Platinum Service Starts with
LEADERS

ONE

Two monks were walking down a country road. They came across a beautiful young girl standing by a muddy stream, afraid to cross it by herself. One monk went over to her, picked her up, and safely carried her over the stream. He returned to his companion and continued on their walk.

After some time, the companion turned to him and said, "What you did was wrong. As monks, we are not allowed to touch women or be in such close proximity to them."

The first monk turned to his companion and said, "I put that girl down when we had crossed the stream. It is you who are still carrying her."

The first monk displayed good leadership, and by being unfettered by rules and formalities, he was able to do what was needed to serve the girl. The second monk was too afraid to break the rules, so he couldn't help the girl. The first monk abandoned all tradition and took control to create an unforgettable moment, as any good leader would.

Before we get into the **five lessons of SPARK**, let's start by exploring the **Platinum Service nucleus** of any great company or organization:

It's crucial that leaders have the courage to do what's right in the moment because they set the example. When a leader models the expected behaviors, the people will follow. That isn't to say exceptional service moments require leaders to break rules. True, sometimes exceptions must be made to solve a problem in the moment. The power leaders give to a **Platinum Service** culture is by demonstrating care for others, a shared purpose, values, and expected behaviors of the overarching service mission. While the first monk bended the guidelines, he showed in the moment what was most important: to put the needs of others first.

Good leaders take three simple action steps that guide them in delivering Platinum Service to both employees and customers.

We will refer to them as

THE "3Cs"

of **Creating a Caring Environment.**

1. Establish a **CULTURE** where everyone matters.

2. Create a deeper **CONNECTION** with team members.

3. SPARK a relationship to create **CUSTOMERS** for life.

And how are these "3 Cs" connected? It comes down to this timeless, evidence-based truth:

CULTURE + CONNECTION + CUSTOMERS
= REVENUE

A leader's objectives will likely always be tied directly or indirectly to profit, or the bottom line, and I don't discount this fact—however, before you focus on the revenue, you must focus on the relationships.

Over the past thirty years, I've worked for six different companies in ten different jobs. I've spoken to 1,600 different organizations in forty-five countries, advised 100+ leaders, and consulted with ten different companies.

In all my experience, I've witnessed firsthand both brilliant and horrible bosses. According to LinkedIn employees, people don't divorce companies, they divorce leaders. It's no different than when there is a disconnect in a marriage relationship. Employees check out mentally and disengage long before physically leaving the company. Many consider this as quitting and staying.

Leaders must model, promote, and apply the same **Platinum Service Mindset (PSM)** they extend to their customers and to the employees they serve. Yes, you read correctly—serve. Rather than a constant pursuit of power, leaders should be the first to exemplify PSM in the workplace by first serving the employees they lead with love and authenticity. Again, that's not a typo. I said "love." Remember, this employer/employee relationship is a marriage and no marriage can thrive without consistent acts of love, both big and small. We demonstrate this love in a business culture by a strong sense of connection to and selfless promotion of the growth of others. Google, for example, is well known for showing the love to their employees. They offer a wide range of perks, from free catered meals to fitness facilities. Google is consistently rated one of the best places to work—not only because of the perks, but because the culture at Google is one that truly promotes employee happiness and growth. The managers take on the role of trusted coach and adviser, focusing on empowering employees and showing interest in their personal growth and well-being. Sundar Pichai, Google's CEO, is beloved by his employees and has a 98 percent approval rating among employees on Glassdoor. The secret? At Google, everyone matters.

Establishing a **culture** where everyone matters and creating deeper connections with team members starts with **Love**. So how do leaders express appreciation and love for their team members? They become emotionologists. In other words, they pay close attention to the emotions of those they serve.

Let's look at a creative example of how to do this. *Undercover Boss,* an Emmy Award-winning CBS television series, is a hugely popular show that is broadcast on international networks in thirty countries. It features senior executives who work undercover in entry-level positions in their own companies to investigate how things are really working. They connect with team members and strive to understand their emotions as well as identify ways the culture and operation can be improved. They use their discoveries to not only enhance their business processes but to reward their hard-working employees in ways that matter. Among the many companies that have been featured are the presidents and chief operating officers of Waste Management, Inc., NASCAR, DirecTV®, Chiquita Brands International, Cinnabon, and Choice Hotels, just to name a few.

I'm convinced that the show is so popular across continents and cultures because of the surprising level of love, authenticity, and connection the bosses express to their employees at the end of each episode. Many of the leaders admit that they'd been out of touch with the challenges—both personal and professional—that employees were facing, and that they'd been disconnected from their own humanity while performing their leadership duties. They admit to being so focused on the bottom line and driving results that they'd ceased to put themselves in the places of the people on the frontline. They'd been so far removed from the day-to-day operations that they couldn't empathize with the real-life obstacles in the corporate culture or work environment that prevented their employees from delivering Platinum Service effectively or consistently. And, sadly, they hadn't demonstrated the principles of Platinum Service to the people who were the heart of the business—their employees.

Establish a **CULTURE** Where
EVERYONE MATTERS

So how can you
ESTABLISH A CULTURE
where everyone believes
that he or she matters
and that they play a vital role in
delivering on **service expectations?**

One company that has established a culture of diversity and inclusivity is Netflix. Besides being a forerunner in technology, Netflix has become known for its diverse programming and inclusive representation featuring diverse casts. Netflix's programming slate actively explores the identities, cultures, and experiences of marginalized groups that don't often get to tell their stories or see their stories mirrored on television in an authentic way. This commitment has opened the brand to a larger consumer base and allowed their company to become globally relevant.

Netflix stated, "It takes diversity of thought, culture, background, and perspective to create a truly global internet TV network." Netflix recognizes that in order to be a successful company, not only did they need to revolutionize their brand and concept, but they needed to create a company that draws on strengths of diverse customer experiences to take their company to the next level.

Intentionally maintaining diversity and inclusion are differentia- tors for creating a successful, global company. Webster's Dictionary states the meaning of culture as it relates to science is "to cultivate and maintain conditions suitable for growth." I firmly believe that cul- ture happens when no one is looking! It's the intangible spirit, the energy of an organization that's sometimes unexplainable.

According to the January-February 2018 issue of the Harvard Business Review:

> "Culture is the tacit social order of an organization: It shapes attitudes and behaviors in wide-ranging and durable ways. Cultural norms define what is encouraged, discouraged, accepted, or rejected within a group. When properly aligned with personal values, drives, and needs, culture can unleash tremendous amounts of energy toward a shared purpose and foster an organization's capacity to thrive."

A Platinum Service culture is created by leaders when they fos- ter random acts of kindness (love) that result in positive emotional experiences for their team members. However, these acts should be anything but random. They are intentional moments of service that become the glue for team loyalty, inclusiveness, and cohesiveness. Tom Bohn, president of the North American Veterinary Community (NAVC), says, "The hardest thing a leader has to do all day is to main- tain culture." Leaders who desire to promote a service-centered cul- ture are purposeful about team bonding; deliver candid, constructive feedback; and provide authentic recognition that appreciates team members who go the extra distance with customers. They understand that culture and values matter just as much as compensation, and that employee engagement and experience are as important as customer experience. Companies with these characteristics stand out as employers and, in return, earn loyalty and passion from their employees. Bohn says, "At NAVC, we have worked hard to create an environment that promotes communication, collaboration, and care. Our kitchen is stocked with the best snacks, the best coffee. There is always something available to energize people. Communal areas are everywhere to share and discuss and debate and bounce ideas around. We put a lot of money into the benefits package. We don't want anyone worrying about their health, or their children's health, or their spouse's health. We want our team members' focus to be on family first, and then the NAVC. We think about it in that order."

When employees feel connected, supported, and valued, conditions are suitable for their commitment and growth toward delivering **SPARK** moments each and every time. Millennials are leading the conversation about what inclusiveness feels like, and smart companies are listening. They've stressed the importance of a culture that's connected to the community in which it serves, and that includes the customer. It's not all about the money. They want to work for businesses that improve the quality of people's lives, and organizations are taking notice.

Kaytie Zimmerman of Forbes.com is a bit of an expert on Millennial preferences in the workplace...because she is one! Zimmerman says that Millennials primarily look for five things from their workplace: benefits that match their values, reason to be loyal, retirement investment options, flexibility to prioritize their lives, and social impact.

When employees feel
connected, supported, and valued,
conditions are suitable for
COMMITMENT AND GROWTH.

Warmth and caring that extends beyond the office walls is another way of building strong communities and creating a company culture where everyone matters. The love that leaders show for their employees should extend to the customers and to the communities. Connections, real connections, result in genuine customer loyalty. In today's information age, earning the trust and respect of customers isn't easy! The competition for products and services is greater every day, and customers have gazillions of choices. Gallup research shows that 70 percent of decision-making is emotion—people who connect with a brand emotionally are more likely to buy more and tell more people. But customer love goes beyond profit margins. Customer love is a way to give back to the community and show your employees that they are working toward a higher purpose.

For example, Olive Garden has teamed up with the American Red Cross to deliver meals in times of need, and they participate in community-wide relations, including "Pasta for Pennies," which benefits the Leukemia & Lymphoma Society. Their parent company's "Darden Harvest" donates food to local food banks on a weekly basis.

Olive Garden recently hosted a "Round Up 4 BGCA" campaign for the Boys & Girls Clubs of America. In this program, every guest was given the opportunity to round up their bill to the nearest dollar, and 100 percent of the proceeds were donated to that nonprofit. These types of community efforts go a long way toward making today's employees feel aligned with something bigger and more far-reaching than the company's bottom line.

When leaders act upon their employee's charitable preferences and demonstrate their commitment to them, they create a culture of both employee and customer love in which teams participate in building communities together and everyone matters. Being intentional about personalizing the experience and anticipating the needs of employees makes team members, internal partners, and stakeholders feel supported and valued. This SPARK of positive energy within an organization becomes infectious and produces a culture of Platinum Service.

Create a
DEEPER CONNECTION
WITH OTHERS

Virgin Group founder Sir Richard Branson said,

> "Succeeding in business is all about making human connections."

Once your culture is established, connection must follow. In large part, culture is about attitudes and actions; connection is about feeling. Remember what Maya Angelou said? People may forget what you said or did, but they won't forget how you made them feel. When that feeling is positive, connection is created. When you create a consistently positive feeling over time, an even deeper connection develops.

> People will forget what you said, people will forget what you did, but they will never forget **HOW YOU MADE THEM FEEL.**
>
> *– Maya Angelou*

While establishing a service-oriented culture begins in new-hire orientation, building connection starts with how leaders welcome new employees to their location. LinkedIn teaches their managers and teams how to genuinely welcome new talent into the workplace. For example, don't say, "This is Sherry. She's great at Excel," but instead, "This is Sherry. She loves tennis. Her passion is writing. She's really going to help us craft our stories, and I'm super excited she's on our team."

How you welcome someone sets the tone for their holistic work experience. It could impact how long they stay with your company or how willing they are to share their ideas. With every decision point and every interaction, you can create a positive feeling. And people will remember the feeling, not your words. They'll remember how you treated them, which will ultimately impact how they treat customers. For example, a young woman began work at a large retail store filling online orders. At the end of her first week on the job, she received a handwritten letter from her boss, welcoming her to the company and offering his support. The employee was taken aback by how meaningful and personalized the note was, and she could tell her boss had put a great deal of thought into it. The note made her day, and gave her an idea. Inspired by her boss, she began leaving short, handwritten notes inside each online order she filled, thanking the customer for their business and telling them to have a great day. The ripple effect of positivity ultimately affected the way the customers viewed the brand.

We operate in a dynamic environment today, and building relationships is no longer limited to making sales calls or having face-to-face meetings. While complex organizational hierarchies, the presence of online platforms, and multiple stakeholders have all made it far more difficult than it used to be, technology has widened connections. Specifically, the internet has created more connections than ever before. Right now, as you're reading this, over 3 billion people are using the internet.

To create a **DEEPER CONNECTION** with your employees, whether live or virtually, you must commit to getting to know them over time—and I mean KNOW THEM WELL.

What are their hopes and dreams for home and at work? What are their fears and concerns? What are their strengths and weaknesses? What is their spouse's name and how old are their children? This may feel like personal overkill for some leaders, so I'll clarify that this isn't about becoming fast friends with every team member. That can be a risk. However, it is about caring enough to be emotionally aware and to show genuine concern for those you work alongside every day. Like it or not, deeper connection is intimate. Intimacy requires a certain amount of vulnerability, which isn't always comfortable. Remember—this is like a marriage and, like any good marriage, a certain level of intimacy is needed for it to work.

And what are the consequences if it doesn't work? MetLife's "Ninth Annual Benefit Trends Study" found that, as the economy slowly rebounds, 36 percent of employees surveyed hoped to work for a different employer in the next twelve months. That's right. These employees are "married" for now but looking for love somewhere else.

People used to spend their entire careers—or at least twenty to thirty years—with one company. These men and women had incredible emotional connections with the companies for which they worked, and the corporate mission statements were imbedded in their hearts and minds. They were loyal to the company, had a passion for its product or service, arrived early, and spent more time at work than at home or building a life outside of work. There was often little separation between what they did professionally and how they defined themselves as people. They were also highly engaged and committed, were married to their jobs and sometimes horrible bosses, for better, for worse, for richer (financial booms), for poorer (hard times), in sickness or in health, to love and to cherish... until retirement, downsizing, or death parted them.

And what did these employees receive in return from their "spouses" (employers or horrible bosses)? At first, they became engaged by the good pay, good benefits, pensions, appreciation, validation, and advancement. But as the Industrial Age gave way to the Information Age, businesses had to change. Corporate reengineering became the golden key to success, and the new mandate from the top of the food chain was, "Do more with less." This meant the rug of corporate marriage and stability was pulled out from under the feet of the loyal souls who were fully engaged.

Just like a marriage between two people, every professional marriage goes through seasons of change—periods of better or worse. However, when the emotional commitment and emotional connection between leader and employee completely and permanently disintegrates, the marriage crumbles and one spouse often goes astray.

As in a marriage, if you're in it for the long haul, creating connection with your people should be a natural part of what you do to build a strong team. That deeper connection makes it easier to see from their point of view when making decisions and reacting to workplace situations. A strong leader will go the extra inch to be intentional in this area. An occasional invitation for lunch or a coffee break—or even taking your fingers off the keyboard to make direct eye contact when an employee or colleague enters your office—can help you create those deep connections. This should be an equal objective to any business goal.

SPARK A RELATIONSHIP
to CREATE CUSTOMERS FOR LIFE

Developing your SPARK as a leader is as much about operating in your own natural gifts, talents, and purpose as it is about creating an unforgettable experience for the customer. When you invest your ability into something meaningful and congruent with your internal wiring, it creates a SPARK, which unleashes pure energy and joy for both you and your customer. You become the SPARK that starts a fire that spreads quickly from person to person, situation to situation, and opportunity to opportunity. Take Steve Jobs, for example. His natural brilliance and skill with all things technological inspired a massive corporation, filled with brilliant, innovative people. His products have changed the way we work, learn, and communicate. But it all started with one man investing his abilities.

DEVELOPING YOUR SPARK

as a leader is as much about **OPERATING IN YOUR OWN NATURAL GIFTS, TALENTS, and PURPOSE** as it is about creating an unforgettable experience for the customer.

On the flip side, the absence of SPARK can prevent you from creating something special. So how does a person or organization find that SPARK? Aristotle said, "Where the needs of the world intersect with your talent, therein lies your vocation."

When I accepted the truth that my purpose is to be fearless and to teach others how to create the future, I found my SPARK and stopped trying to be like everyone else. At times, I'd lost my sense of self because I thought I had to say everything exactly right so that customers would hire me and others would value me. Now I know how wrong that is! When you find your inner SPARK, it allows your mojo, your essence, and your swag to fill a room. How? Simply put, you are no longer in the room; the room is in you, and that's when you become immersed in the moment. You exist to give instead of to get. Your SPARK becomes the push, the nudge, the shove that everyone—especially your customers—needs to find their own inner SPARK.

Bruce Barton, one of the founders of BBDO, one of the nation's largest advertising agencies, said it best. "If you have anything really valuable to contribute to the world, it will come through the expression of your personality, that single SPARK of divinity that sets you off and makes you different from every other living creature."

• • •

There was a time when I lost my SPARK. As positive as my experience was with the Walt Disney Company, one day I found myself completely empty, and I walked away from my job as sales and new business development director of the world-renowned Disney Institute at Walt Disney World Resort. I left a guaranteed paycheck and benefits galore. In this role, I had wanted for nothing and had been on the fast track to a bright career.

Even though I was living my own version of the American Dream, something was missing. There was a hole in my soul, a gap in my mind, and a sense of being stuck in neutral. One day, it just didn't click for me anymore. It had worked until it didn't work anymore, and I knew I couldn't fake it.

Professionally, I was content but not happy. I was successful on the outside but felt insignificant on the inside. I was simply going through the motions because I'd settled for a chair, a check, and a cup of coffee in the cubicle farm. There was a hole in my soul, a gap in my mind, and a sense of being stuck in neutral and going nowhere fast. One day I reached a point where it just didn't click anymore. You can't deliver Platinum Service to your customers when you're at this point. This is when it's time to move on and find your SPARK elsewhere.

Where there is no SPARK, there is no joy. Where there is no joy, there is no hope; and where there is no hope, there is no passion. Without passion, a job is just a job. A business is simply something to do instead of something that makes a difference in the world. And a customer is just one more thing to handle. But when you find your SPARK, you find your joy, and when you find your joy, you find freedom. And when you find freedom, you find your chutzpah. Without this, you can't help anybody.

But when you find your SPARK you find **YOUR JOY**, and when you find your joy, you find **FREEDOM**. And when you find freedom, YOU FIND YOUR CHUTZPAH.

Without this, you can't help anybody.

Be the SPARK. Create the SPARK. Get moving and, for goodness' sake, don't stay stuck on a bridge to nowhere! Somewhere in the world, someone or something needs your SPARK. All you have to do is create a culture of Platinum Service delivered with a brilliant touch.

EMOTIONAL COMMITMENT
is FOUR TIMES as valuable as rational commitment
in driving discretionary effort.

(Source: Corporate Leadership Counsel and Brilliant Service)

Think about what it means to be a practicing Emotionologist!

1. **Describe in words, symbols, or pictures what you're doing and what your people are doing and saying.**

2. **What is the impact of these words and actions on your service culture?**

3. **What is the impact of these words and actions on your customer experience?**

EMOTIONOLOGY
emotion + | -ology
The art and science of making memorable moments for every guest.

RECOMMENDATIONS

CULTURE

Encourage employees to do the right things at the right time when no one is looking. Reward this behavior often and model it at every turn.

CONNECTION

This is the emotional glue that empowers your talent to exceed customer expectations, not because they have to but because they want to. Extend an invitation to get to know your individual team members better. Put at least one such invitation on your calendar per month. Afterward, show that you've listened by following up on something they told you, like writing a good luck note for their son's big championship soccer match.

CUSTOMERS

With just a swipe of their fingers, today's educated and demanding customers can let the world know if your brand is one that they know, like, trust, and will recommend to others. Be intentional about branding customer moments and creating that unforgettable SPARK. Also, be quick about recovery experiences when necessary. Resolve problems promptly and with enthusiasm. Go the extra inch!

Don't just respond to customer requests; anticipate their needs. Turn a casual mention into an opportunity to surprise and delight them. Note how often you're doing it, so you can measure your intention. Follow up with a handwritten note later.

Take the time to experience the customer's journey. Have a customer experience walk-through this week and commit to at least one customer experience per week/month/quarter.

"

"I have learned to imagine
an invisible sign around
each person's neck that says,
'Make me feel important!'"

— Mary Kay Ash, Founder,
Mary Kay Cosmetics

CHAPTER

SEE
Them as **Guests**

TWO

SPARK begins and ends with how you see your customers, colleagues, and employees. Creating customers for life doesn't happen by accident; you must show up consistently and exceed their expectations. You have to unlearn what you've been taught about customer service and begin to **see people—all of them—as guests**, rather than customers, employees, or suppliers. Regardless of what industry you are in, your customers are the key drivers behind every business decision. They are the reason we all have our jobs. Customers are all your business patrons, all your clients. Because you want to meet their needs and make them feel comfortable, they are, of course, your guests. But your guests extend beyond patrons. Everyone who walks through the door, expected or not, is your guest, even if they choose not to do business with you. Just like I was treated when I first entered the Ritz as a young man, everyone, regardless of whether they're a diner, shopper, or registered guest of your brand, should be welcomed into your business and treated with the utmost respect.

Rolex, a Swiss watch company, certainly has a global reputation for excellence and royal treatment of their customers. Matthew Becker, one of the largest sellers of Rolex, said of the success during his 20-year experience, "It could be a $10 gemstone we sold twenty years ago, it doesn't matter what they bought, we'll do whatever we can to make the customer happy."

Becker credits his authentic passion for customer service as the foundation of the brand's success. He recommends that all business owners treat their customers like family. Rolex's maintenance of treating their customers as respected guests has helped this brand become a household name and maintain itself as No. 2 in Forbes' "World's 100 Most Reputable Companies" list.

Your employees are also your guests. They show up every day, don't they? They are guests because they spend time in your establishment and, because you care about them, you want to ensure they feel welcome, valued, and have a pleasant experience. Even suppliers with whom you interact frequently deserve to be welcomed and honored. Relationships are the currency of the future. An authentic connection is the key to lasting relationships with both your internal and external guests. This is how you create long-term retention and repeat business because wherever they go, they carry you with them.

YOU HAVE TO UNLEARN
what you've been taught about
CUSTOMER SERVICE
and begin to see people—all of them
—as **GUESTS**, rather than customers,
colleagues, or employees.

Seeing customers as guests comes down to making a warm connection. According to a Bain & Company study, 60 percent to 80 percent of customers who describe themselves as satisfied don't do more business with a company that initially satisfied them. How can that be? Often it's due to a lack of connection. In fact, disconnection is the reason why so many one-time sales that are completely satisfying never translate into lifetime customer value.

So what can you do to "CONNECT?"

I was invited by the executive team of New Jersey's Kennedy Health—one of the nation's leading healthcare systems—to spend time with 270 of their leaders. While there, I asked Joe Devine, president and CEO, for permission to share this heartwarming story about a nurse who had treated one of their patients as a guest.

> Last week, I was assigned a patient in the Coronary Care Unit. Her condition was grave and hospice was suggested.
>
> Thirty years earlier, she had emigrated from Poland to work as a pharmacist in a chemical plant. But she'd been keeping a secret from her friends: Her son was incarcerated in Pennsylvania. She hadn't seen or heard his voice for eighteen months.
>
> Over the next several hours, her friend, the other hospital staff, a judge, prison attendants, and I all worked together to arrange a call between my patient and

her son. Eventually, the prison called me to discuss the matter. The superintendent agreed to try to arrange a video conference, but said it would take time because they had to go through the appropriate channels. Time was something we didn't have much of, but phone calls were made and transferred, technology was frantically acquired and set up, and many prayers were said.

We waited for permission from the prison and finally got the okay for a phone call at noon. When my patient heard her son's voice, she talked in Polish nonstop for five minutes. The call ended thirty minutes later with my patient hugging the iPad and trying to kiss her son.

This moment would NEVER have happened if a lot of people hadn't sacrificed hours from their workday to assist me in granting this woman's last wish.

We started her on comfort care at 3:00 p.m. the same day, and she was able to pass peacefully."

— MAGGIE MAE, RN CMSRN, Cherry Hill ICU

This nurse and her colleagues created a real connection. Not just a literal one between a dying mother and her estranged yet beloved son, but figuratively speaking as well. This brilliant and compassion-ate nurse worked tirelessly to make something special happen, creating a once-in-a-lifetime moment.

Treating people like a guest entails gracious hospitality. For example, if a customer comes to visit you in your home office or a local coffee spot, offer them a refreshment. Be sure they're comfortable – offer them the best seat in the house. Give them your undivided attention. Don't interrupt, don't look down at your cell phone or type on your iPad. Show customers they are special by tuning the rest of the world out and focusing on them. Gracious hospitality comes down to good, old-fashioned manners. Hospitality is making people feel good while exploring your products or services and making them feel "at home." Let's look at a few examples.

The Disney Vacation Club follows a signature "Welcome Home," and this is how they greet every member, in any location. Beyond the resorts offering features that reflect the comfort and conveniences of home, their employees are trained and committed to making Guests feel like there truly is "no place like home." Even their selling process differs from the rest—there's no hard sell, or sign-on-the-line pressure—just a fun tour, scoop of complimentary ice cream, and a commemorative photo to remember the magic of your experience. Talk about branded moments!

Lindsay Lacy of Lindsay Elizabeth Photography in Richmond, Texas, invites her customers to her home-based studio so they can have a more personalized experience. "I want to give my clients a really great experience, and I want them to look back on their images [years from now] and love them," Lacy said. "I also try to be a little more than the person who just shows up to take pictures."

Mary Lou DuBois has championed the "Culture of Care" at Provision Healthcare, and they consider the cancer patient's perspective in everything that touches their experience. This includes both tangible and intangible things. They have beautiful outdoor landscaping, an easy walkway to the entrance, easy navigation on campus, a parking lot rather than a garage, beautiful interior design, comfortable furniture, a non-clinical atmosphere and environment, a friendly and welcoming check-in process, respectful and timely communication, and patient-focused operational flow. In other words, they see their patients as guests.

As Provision Healthcare grew, Mary Lou visited many other leading and well-established medical providers. She noted that the traditional model—sterile environment, clinically focused staff, and operational efficiencies that serve the provider, not the patient—was the norm. But that approach contradicted her deep-rooted Culture of Care values and, she believed, compromised the cancer patient's experience and quality of their care.

Her vision was to create a world-class patient experience, which is now a brand differentiator for Provision Healthcare. This significant change impacts the overall patient experience before, during, and after their treatment.

Whenever a cancer patient finishes their treatment, they ring the victory bell in the Provision CARES Proton Therapy Center lobby in Knoxville, Tennessee. The bell was rung by the first graduating patient on February 18, 2014.

Ring this bell.
Three times well;
Its toll to clearly say,
My treatment's done.
This course is run;
AND I AM ON MY WAY!

Their patients express their appreciation at their graduation ceremony when they ring the bell. At that time, the staff is reminded of the value of life, the vulnerability of the cancer patients, and the tremendous privilege, honor, and reward it is to serve them and their families.

• • •

- What is your version of a victory bell for your customers?
- How are you treating them like guests?

There's a shift happening
ALL OVER THE WORLD,
and delivering **GREAT CUSTOMER SERVICE**
simply doesn't cut it anymore.

You must deliver Platinum Service, and that includes seeing your customers like guests. So what are ways to do this?

START With Your
EMPLOYEES

As you onboard new people, it's important to take the time to tell them the story of your business. They aren't just providing a service to support your business; they're now a critical part of the story and represent you as much as you represent them. See these newly talented contributors as guests and make sure they know the big picture and where they fit in. Tom Bohn at NAVC says that it would be a big mistake to assume that new hires automatically understand how to provide excellent customer service. So, he makes customer service a key part of their training even though they are hired for positions in the veterinary field. He says, "At NAVC, we always train our people to find a way to get to 'yes' with the customer and make them feel good about the experience. We're going to have errors and mistakes, but we need to find a path forward and make sure each and every customer walks away from the interaction feeling good about it."

GIVE a Little
"EXTRA"

I once shared the stage with a *New York Times* columnist, and he told a story about going to breakfast with his best friend. They placed their order for pancakes and a side dish of fruit. When their food was served, the waitress made it a point to let them know that she had given both of them extra fruit. She didn't have to do that, and yet she did. As a result, she was rewarded with a 50 percent tip! What can you do to make sure that you give your guests a little something extra every day?

DISCOVER Your
CUSTOMER'S JOURNEY

Map out your critical customer touchpoints (both live and virtual) and assess how you are treating them at each interaction. Do they feel like guests? Determine if all the touchpoints "add up" to Platinum Service. A recent article from management consulting firm McKinsey & Company says, "It's not enough to make customers happy with each individual interaction." In one of their customer-experience surveys of 27,000 American consumers across fourteen different industries, McKinsey found that effective customer journeys—or a cluster of interactions are more important than individual interactions. Clusters of interaction come directly from a customer's experience of consistency from a company: customer journey, emotional and communication consistency. Measuring satisfaction on customer journeys is 30 percent more predictive of overall customer satisfaction than measuring happiness for each individual interaction.

WALK A MILE
in Your CUSTOMER'S SHOES

In other words, shop your own product. How do your people handle each transaction or service breakdown? Are they seeing each moment as an opportunity to create a "guest moment?" Is there a better way? How many touchpoints are there with the customer?

Use **YOUR**
CUSTOMER'S NAME

As simple as it might sound, most people like to hear the sound of their own name. According to research, small-business employees only ask for the customer's name 21 percent of the time during a customer service interaction...but 86 percent of customers said they enjoy when business employees refer to them by name.

Dale Carnegie once said,

> "If you remember my name, you pay me a subtle compliment; you indicate that I have made an impression on you. Remember my name and you add to my feeling of importance."

In their first encounter, brand that first critical moment by introducing yourself, getting their name, and greeting them by it each time!

A great way to understand your customers' thoughts and feelings around your business is to use Net Promoter Score® (NPS) to measure the customer experience. You calculate your NPS by asking customers one key question: "Using a scale of 0-10, how likely is it that you would recommend this company/service to a friend or colleague?" Respondents are grouped by their scores—Promoters (9-10), Passives (7-8), and Detractors (0-6). Subtracting the percentage of your Detractors from your Promoters gives you your Net Promoter Score.

Behind all the numbers lies some useful and important information. At the end of the day, an NPS can tell you whether people are loyal and enthusiastic about your company, or whether they are unhappy. Knowing this information can lead to changes in company culture and service mindset.

Virgin Media chose to work with Satmetrix, a Net Promoter company, to launch a program to rally their 14,000 employees around a common goal: to focus on the customer first. Since then, they've seen an 18-point rise in their NPS, a 20 percent reduction in customer churn levels, a 6.4 percent increase in customers buying multiple services, and several other process improvements. By taking a customer-centered approach and seeing their customers as guests, Virgin Media saw dramatic improvements company wide.

• • •

Think about how you anticipate unspoken needs, and be the SPARK for your employees, colleagues, suppliers, or customers in your day-to-day routine. I believe it is part of our DNA to help someone who can do nothing for us. Will you be a SPARK for someone today?

You can start by
SEEING THEM AS GUESTS.

CHAPTER

PERSONALIZE
the Experience

THREE

Here's one prediction I can make with confidence: In the future, you'll be paid for the experiences you create and the difference you make. And guess what? The future is right now.

Simply meeting demands and sticking to a tried-and-true formula won't cut it these days. Your customers have unique and varied personalities, so your customer service approach has to be uniquely personalized to suit each one. Something we have learned recently about small-business customer service statistics from research conducted by several sources is that 38 percent of small-business customers say "personalization" is what creates a happy customer experience. In Platinum Service speak, "personalizing the experience" means to make a positive first and lasting impression by giving each customer very individual or "VIP" treatment to create satisfaction and rewarding relationships. In your business and in life, you must be unforgettable. Being unforgettable is essential, and the good news is that it's also attainable.

Simply meeting demands and sticking to a tried-and-true formula won't cut it these days. Your **CUSTOMERS** have unique and varied **PERSONALITIES,** so your customer service approach has to be uniquely personalized to suit each one.

Let me share an example with you. I was flying from San Francisco to Columbus, Ohio one evening during the unfavorable winter season and had a quick stop to change planes in Detroit. As fate would have it, my connecting flight was canceled. I thought,

"Hey, no sweat. I'll just catch the next flight."

It was scheduled to leave four hours later, at 7:35 p.m., and was the last flight of the day.

It was Detroit, it was winter, and the weather conditions didn't improve, so the next flight was also canceled. Now I was in a bit of a panic because I had a full day of meetings the next day with Cardinal Health—a $91 billion healthcare services company.

My frustration and anxiety incited me to make a knee-jerk decision to rent a car and drive the three-and-a-half hours through snow and ice to Columbus. I called my favorite aunt who had moved to Detroit and, being a traditional Southern woman, she said,

"Come on by and have dinner before you hit the road."

I am so glad that I did! I was able to enjoy an awesome meal before the long, frigid drive.

I finally hit the road, plugged in my iPod so I could blast some old-school tunes, and jammed on down the road. I arrived at my hotel at 2:00 a.m. exhausted, missing my family, and without luggage.

The next morning, I hit my Yelp app to find the closest men's clothing store. There was no way I was going to a meeting with key executives looking travel worn, smelling musty, and seeming like I'd just rolled out of bed.

> "You look frumpy. Image is everything,"

I could hear my teen daughter's voice saying in my head. My biggest fashion and image critic, she'd be screaming,

> "Get it together, Dad! You can't talk about platinum and look tarnished!"

Thank goodness I was staying at the Hilton Columbus at Easton across from Easton Town Center, a shopping paradise outside Columbus, Ohio. I scrolled through Yelp for a listing of all the men's stores. I looked at my watch. It was 8:28 a.m., and my first meeting was at 10:30 a.m. Big problem: the stores didn't open until 10:00 a.m. I called a few of them, biting my nails and hoping that one of them would be open early on a Monday morning. No luck. Then, I noticed that there was a Nordstrom—a full-fledged retail store—nearby. I dialed the number, and my call was immediately answered by a live person.

I explained my situation and was transferred to Trina, a manager at Nordstrom Easton Town Center. I told her that I had a very important meeting with an important client who was thirty minutes away, and I needed to be professionally outfitted. She asked for my pant, shirt, shoe, and suit jacket size and told me to head right over. She said she'd open the store at 8:45 a.m. so I could buy what I needed. At this point, you can bet I was feeling the Nordstrom love. I felt like a very important person. Talk about a positive first impression.

When I got there, the security team rolled up the metal door like it was a red carpet. There to greet me with a warm, hearty handshake was Melissa, Trina's assistant, and Armaan, my personal shopper for the next forty-five minutes. Armaan had received my sizes and color preferences from Trina and had already laid out an ensemble for me in the men's dressing room. He said they had a tailor on site who could quickly hem my pants and take in my jacket.

From there, my experience got even better. During this brief exchange, Armaan noticed my dry skin—a.k.a. ash attack—and placed a bottle of Jack Black Industrial Strength Hand Healer with Vitamins A & E on the counter for me to use. Yes, that was some serious Nordstrom love.

As I paid for everything, he said he had some cologne testers to give me, and in that split second, I heard Pharrell Williams' "Happy" soundtrack playing in my head. In a pinch, Nordstrom totally took care of me. One hour later, I went to my meeting at Cardinal Health looking good, smelling good, and imagining my daughter saying,

> "You look good, Dad."

Nordstrom found a way to connect with me and win my loyalty. I was so excited about the experience that I posted a selfie of Armaan, Trina, and myself on Twitter and Instagram. Within two minutes of my posting, I received a reply from Nordstrom's "mother ship" that said: "We are thrilled to hear you had a great experience at our Nordstrom Easton Town Center location, Simon! Thanks for sharing."

Nordstrom's had me from "Hello." In other words, they created a positive first impression by opening the store for me and working to personalize their service and product recommendations in my time of need. You've probably heard the old adage: you don't get a second chance to make a first impression. When it comes to customer interactions, nothing could be truer! Here are a few things to keep in mind:

- **A customer's first impression of you or your business is formed in the first few seconds!**

- **The moment of truth starts when the speaking starts!**

While this may be the case, if you are interacting face-to-face with customers, bear in mind that our communication consists of 93 percent body language and only 7 percent words, so be sure to use open, positive gestures.

When it comes to **ENSURING A POSITIVE FIRST IMPRESSION,** you know the basic
"DO'S" & "DON'TS."

THE DON'TS...

- **Don't look past the customer;** look right at them.

- **Avoid crossing your arms** because it makes you look unapproachable.

- **Be sure not to convey an uninterested attitude** by looking down at your phone or computer or task at hand when a customer approaches you.

NOW FOR THE DO'S...

- **Do begin by welcoming someone in a warm, sincere way.** Greetings are very important!

- **Do the easy things such as smiling, making eye contact, offering a firm but friendly handshake,** and even if you are on the phone and customers can't see you, be sure to smile and be open and personable.

- **Be sure to have good posture.** Using appropriate body language and tone will add conviction to your well-chosen words!

Always
BE MINDFUL
of your message.

Regardless of your type of business, your choice of words has a significant effect on how others perceive you. Personalizing service includes using words that resonate with your customer. People with varying experiences and backgrounds communicate differently. New parents don't speak the same language as rock stars. Seasoned retirees don't talk like Millennials. The best thing to do is to follow the lead of the other person. Research shows that the difference between getting—or keeping—a customer comes down to the words we use. All conversations with customers should be positive, personalized, and help build a relationship between them and your organization.

BE CAREFUL
not to make assumptions
and, of course, avoid speaking
down to someone.

You don't want to patronize. Yet at the same time, you don't want to alienate customers by using words that are too elevated. A friend of mine told me about a recent experience she had with a retailer. After making her way to the checkout counter with her purchases, she encountered a rude cashier who didn't make eye contact, much less exchange any pleasantries. After her items had been rung up, my friend swiped her debit card, and to her surprise, heard a loud beep from the machine. "Your card has been declined," the cashier said loudly, drawing looks from nearby customers. "Could you swipe it again?" said my friend, who had made a purchase with this same card only hours ago. "Honey, it's not the machine—you don't have enough money," said the cashier. My friend was appalled! She left her items at the counter and walked out of the store. Later, she sent an email to the store's customer service department, saying they wouldn't have her business again. The thing that made her the most angry? The cashier had called her "honey," and spoke to her in a condescending tone in front of the other customers. Using respectful language and treating your customers, first and foremost, as people is key in delivering Platinum Service.

PERSONALIZING
the customer experience
gives you the ability to form-fit a positive experience to your individual customers.

Customers feel more comfortable when they are respected and included. One way we can do this is to be intuitive. It's essential to remember that when serving customers, personalizing your approach by embracing diversity will keep them coming back. An associate of mine witnessed a brief glimpse of such a customer encounter in a Macy's. She was browsing through a Macy's perfume and cologne counter when she saw a woman, wearing a hijab, approach a MAC Cosmetics counter. The employee at the counter greeted her with a smile and they spoke briefly. While the employee chose a few products for this customer, another employee began tucking tissues into the edges of the customer's hijab to protect it from the makeup. Now, every time our associate goes to a MAC counter, she remembers that customer's smile —and that customer will likely always re-member when two employees were considerate and kind enough to customize their service approach and adapt to her needs.

As I've mentioned, words can make you stand out against your competition. And words are what others will remember THE MOST about you. Did you know there are more than a million words in the English language and we only use between 2,000 and 2,500? That's right, we generally limit our daily vocabulary to between two hun-dred and three hundred words! I think my young daughter already knows about a thousand more words than I do, but I always try to increase my vocabulary in order to connect with all my customers and personalize how I treat them.

CHALLENGE YOURSELF
to SPEAK MORE EFFECTIVELY.

Avoid using words that are over-used such as "like" and "very." First, you don't want to sound like everyone else. Secondly, some av-erage words don't always carry your intended message. And lastly, you want to engage your customer. You want to be interesting!

To come across in a Platinum, personal way, avoid impersonal— or sloppy—language. This creates a barrier between you and your customer.

Using phrases such as these does not show care or respect for a customer:

- **Who's calling?**

- **Are you in our system?**

- **Hang on.**

- **She's busy.**

- **She's in a meeting.**

- **Let me pull you up ...**

- **"Yep" or "Yeah."**

- **Waddya need?**

- **You guys.**

- **Sorta.**

- **"Um" or "Ah."**

- **OMG/LOL.**

You might be wondering,

> "What if most of my customer interactions ARE online vs. face-to-face? Do first impressions and word choice still matter?"

You bet! As of a few years ago, 88.5 percent of the United States population uses the internet. We live in an information age aided by technology, so emails, texts, tweets—they can all work to your advantage in reaching your customers. Just beware that with email and other electronic forms of communication, messages send faster than our brains compute!

On average, there are over 6 billion text messages sent every day in the U.S. and 500 million tweets sent via Twitter worldwide. With this kind of constant communication, language is bound to change. David Crystal, a renowned British linguist, wrote in his book, *The Stories of English,* about how modern technology has affected language. He says email, texting, and "netspeak" have all visibly changed the way we interact with language, and that the internet has rapidly sped up the evolution of language. Online, users tend to shorten their conversations by using cyberspeak such as BRB and LOL as well as emojis. While the internet can connect millions of people, it can also depersonalize us as people, leading to a less personal experience overall.

To avoid these potentially alienating moments, think of these **three Cs** of personalizing your virtual service communication: **clear, comprehensive,** and **considerate.**

Make sure your website is customer friendly and creates a favorable first impression. It should be clear who you are and what you do. Contact information should be readily available and easy to find. Communicate with the customer on their level; avoid phrases with heavy jargon or ambiguous meanings. For example, if you're in retail, you might be familiar with acronyms like KPI, POS, and ATV. While Key Performance Indicator, Point of Sale, and Average Transaction Value are important phrases in your industry, this "alphabet soup" means nothing to your customers and won't capture their attention or their business. Be considerate of the person on the other end of the exchange. If you're only encountering customers in cyberspace, make sure they know they're valued on their first click!

Beyond the words you use, make sure the platform is customer friendly as well. Virgin America knows how to show their customers they are valued, just by their website design. Now an airline company is not the first kind of business I think of when I think of customer-friendly websites. However, Virgin America's website has been praised as one of the most accessible and responsive websites in the airline industry. When a customer opens the website, they are greeted with a statement, "Your world just got bigger"–a big promise to make. Underneath that promise are three menus that let you choose your number of guests, where you're departing from, and where you're going. By using a simple, easy-to-use home screen, customers don't have to search for what they're looking for. Virgin America finds it for them.

Another company that does it right is Big Cartel. Big Cartel claims to offer "simple tools and resources to build a unique online store, manage and sell [artists'] work, delight their fans and customers, and run their business their own way." Other than having a visually stunning website, Big Cartel's site hosts simple navigation and educational videos that display what a customer can expect from Big Cartel's services. Their website-making software is acclaimed to be intuitive and easy to use, even by beginners. By showcasing their products in a visually appealing way, Big Cartel is not only selling themselves well, they are reassuring their customers that their services are worth their money.

If most of your customer interactions are by phone, follow the same guidelines about language and friendliness to ensure a favorable first impression.

Here are some tips to help ensure each service moment is Platinum!

- **Mind the length of greetings and voicemails.**

- **Speak slowly and clearly.**

- **Leave your name and company, contact number, and a brief message.**

- **If you can't maintain 24-hour live support, create an after-hours automated attendant greeting.**

- **Tell your callers when you're closed and ask them to call back.**

- **Put a SMILE in your voice!**

TO BE THE

take a few minutes to reflect on these questions.

1. **Consider when someone enters your workspace.**

   - How do you greet them?

   - What does the area look like?

   - What do YOU look like?

2. **What does your WORD CHOICE reflect about you and your brand?**

3. **Are your phone greeting and website positive? What could improve?**

While first impressions and language are key, personalizing your Platinum Service doesn't end there. The quality of service you deliver is five times more important in influencing purchase decisions than a product's features, performance, and even price. When you combine the unique strengths of people with technology, you can give each customer what he wants— whether it's efficiency, information, advice, social contact, or anonymity. Recent research revealed that 75,000 people who interacted with contact-center representatives or used self-service channels found that over-the-top efforts made little difference. All that customers really want is to be treated like a VIP and have their problems solved by people who care about their needs.

A great example is Chewy.com, an online service that offers a variety of brands of pet food, and delivers them to your door. The service is personal from the start, allowing you to choose exactly the right food for your pet. However, their **SPARK** doesn't stop there. One customer unexpectedly lost her dog. In her grief, she forgot to cancel her Chewy.com subscription, and her auto-shipment arrived just days after the tragic event. She contacted customer service to see if there was any way she could return the food. Chewy.com customer service exceeded her expectations. Not only did she receive a full refund for the food, but the next day, a van pulled up to her house with a bouquet of flowers and a bereavement card, courtesy of Chewy.com. They expressed condolences and asked the customer to please donate the unused food to a local shelter. Talk about personal service! The customer was so touched, she wrote back, saying that Chewy.com would receive all her business in the future.

As this example shows, personal service is not about treating everyone the same. Some people, like the grieving customer, need a little extra care and attention. Others simply want to know that they are seen as an individual. Once, after checking into a hotel, room service delivered a nice assortment of cheeses and some wine. Lovely, right? The problem was that anyone who knows me knows I'd much rather have milk and cookies—snack food. So I sent the wine and cheese back and told them my personal preferences. Later, I returned to my room and found a wonderful assortment of Zapp's Potato Chips and soft drinks. I savored every single bag of those amazing chips and thought about the great service at that hotel the whole time. What started out as nice became more. It became a personalized moment.

Here are some
ADDITIONAL THINGS TO DO to DELIVER a
PERSONALIZED EXPERIENCE:

1. **Hire for attitude and train for success.** Training can't fix what human resources doesn't catch. Trina, Melissa, and Armaan from Nordstrom's all possessed customer-focused attitudes and went above and beyond to provide Platinum Service.

2. **Have a live, happy, glad-to-be-at-work person answer your phone ninety minutes prior to your store's posted opening hours.** Can you imagine how thankful I was that someone answered the phone that cold February morning?!

3. **Capture the moment via digital photo** with the customer's permission and post to social media.

4. **Retweet to extend the life of this social proof** to an entire audience of people online.

Personal service is about seeing your customers as INDIVIDUALS, with their own set of wants, needs, and preferences.

Creating a personal moment will provide a SPARK that changes their customer experience.

"

"Brands and individuals
who offer radically
superior customer service
stand out because they
anticipate unexpressed
needs or wishes."

— Carmine Gallo, communications expert

CHAPTER

ANTICIPATE
and **Uncover Needs**

FOUR

You may think that you can deliver customer service by using common sense. However, the Platinum Service that we deliver through SPARK is anything but common. We remember the unique and unquestionably exquisite experiences that take our breath away. These rare occasions become locked in our minds. This is how word-of-mouth information spreads like wildfire and a hidden gem becomes an overnight sensation. The brands that come to mind are Zappos, Pinkberry, and the Fairmont Grand Del Mar hotel in San Diego.

The flip side is true as well. Poor, inconsistent, sloppy service also sends a message. It says, "We don't care about you, and it really doesn't matter if you return or not. We have enough business to keep us going." That's the attitude that I sense from some organizations that refuse to shift.

The hungry, aggressive, take-no-prisoner types of businesses are

INVESTING

in their people first

and their product second.

Success in today's competitive business environment is contingent on predicting and understanding customer behavior—and customizing solutions to suit their needs. It's about anticipating and uncovering needs. By actively listening and observing, as well as noting patterns and recurring needs and questions, you can begin to "know"—or at least anticipate—what your customers need—before they even ask.

I was speaking at a convention in Los Angeles and I asked someone who worked at the venue a question. He looked me in the eye and said, "I don't know." Wow, what a caring response. It was already a less-than-Platinum moment, but the conversation quickly slid downhill when he said, "I'm with a third-party company and that's not our job." I made a mental note to not use his company in the future.

Across town at the Beverly Wilshire Hotel, I had the opposite experience. I had just finished a meeting with a prospective client and asked the waiter for the bill. He said, "Would you like me to call valet and have your car brought around?" Now, that's Platinum Service with a brilliant touch! He anticipated my need and exceeded my expectations.

Your customers have
two types of needs:
SPOKEN AND
UNSPOKEN.

Spoken needs are expressed. The customer actually tells you what they need, like I did with the guy at the convention center. Unspoken needs must be uncovered by active listening, observing clues, and asking high-level questions. And that's what the waiter at the Beverly Wilshire did. To deliver Platinum Service, you must respond to both.

When you're able to anticipate what a customer might do based on who they are and what they may be concerned about, you create a branded moment. And you are better able to engage them in a conversation about their needs. This brings me to an important point. When it comes to uncovering needs, ask customers what they need before they have to ask YOU! It's one thing to show your willingness to help customers when they do have questions, but if you ask customers what they need before they ask, they begin to perceive you as a helpful partner. This could be as simple as a waiter refilling your glass before you ask or bringing ketchup with your French fries, to something as impressive as a hotel knowing you have an early meeting and leaving fresh coffee outside your door in the morning. Even Netflix, like I mentioned earlier, and YouTube show they anticipate customer needs by tailoring your homepage to suit your preferences.

Sometimes, to anticipate and uncover your customer's unspoken needs, you're going to have to dig a little. Consider these suggestions:

- **Listen to what the customer is not saying.**

- **Read between the lines.**

- **Listen beyond the words.**

- **Give them time to express themselves.**

- **Ask questions to ensure understanding.**

- **Notice expressions, words, and tone of voice.**

- **Watch and listen for emotional indicators such as folding their arms, rolling their eyes, smiling, or expressing confusion.**

- **Be aware of your biases, and suspend prejudgments.**

There are also some things you can do to make your customer happy BEFORE you even meet them. **Research the customer as a person; look into their industry; and investigate their company.** Essentially, you want to do some homework! And guess what? They're doing THEIR homework, too! According to the small-business customer service statistics...

58 percent of Americans conduct
ONLINE RESEARCH
about the small-business products and
services they are thinking about purchasing.

Here are some tools to use to learn more
ABOUT YOUR CUSTOMER:

- LinkedIn

- Facebook

- Twitter

- Instagram

- YouTube

- Company website bios

- Their assistant

- Google

- **Glassdoor.com** (voice of the employee)

Social media is a great way to learn about your customers, especially because—according to research—online adults, aged 18-34, are most likely following a brand via social networking - about 95 percent! This comes as no surprise when you consider that 93 percent of companies that use social media to market their products and services regularly use Facebook ads. The average consumer mentions brands ninety times a week with family, friends, and co-workers. Take a look at the following list. Consider the possibilities of what you can learn from these cyber outlets:

- **What they Tweet**

- **What they post on Facebook**

- **Their "Likes"**

- **Shared photos**

- **"Friends"**

- **LinkedIn connections or discussions**

Listening to customers through social media can not only help you understand your customers' tastes, it can also help you improve your service. Take Domino's Pizza, for example. In 2010, Domino's suffered a major PR disaster when a video of employees using contaminated ingredients on the pizzas went viral. Even before the video, Domino's was facing harsh customer criticism about the taste of their pizza, and customer satisfaction ratings were low. After hundreds of negative comments on social media, Domino's took action. Firstly, they did something surprising—they admitted their product was bad. Then, they launched the Pizza Turnaround campaign, in which they spent millions of dollars acknowledging their problem and reinventing their pizza "from the crust up." They promoted their comeback widely on social media, and even filmed a short documentary about the process to have full transparency with their customers. The result was a 14.3 percent jump in sales, and an ongoing dialogue with their customers online. So what's the moral? Domino's used social media to listen to their customers' wants, needs, and feedback—even when that feedback was bad—and then took action to improve.

When you have learned what you can about the customer, it's helpful to research their industry as well. What types of trends impact their world? Consider some of these categories when doing your research to anticipate possible needs.

Trends that Impact Their World:

- **Economic**

- **Market/Business**

- **Technology**

- **Government**

- **Global**

- **Target customer**

REFLECTION:
ANTICIPATE NEEDS

1. CONSIDER A CURRENT PROSPECT.

What tools and topics can you use to learn about:

- **Their personal interests and needs?**

- **Their industry?**

- **Their company?**

2. LIST THREE THINGS YOU ALREADY KNOW ABOUT THEM.

When it comes to uncovering needs, did you know that the quality of your questions determines the quality of the answers you receive? I like to tell my clients to ask "high level" questions. These types of questions dig beyond the surface to get to the heart of the matter. They inspire critical thinking and spur interesting, thoughtful conversation. Most importantly, they show that you value the customer enough to go deeper to discover what they truly need.

FOLLOW THIS PATH
to cut to the chase
of what a customer needs:

1. The first step is **ensuring that a customer is open to your questions,** so position your question.

2. Once you have your customer's permission to begin asking questions, **probe to understand their "big picture" requirements.**

3. Then get down to the nitty gritty. **Ask questions that are more specific and focus on the details of the needs.**

4. Next, **clarify and confirm.** These questions demonstrate to the customer that you have a complete understanding of their needs. These questions leave no doubt in their mind that you have listened intently to the details that they have provided.

And finally, **question to differentiate.** Ask astute questions to demonstrate that you are really thinking—and that you are dedicated to ensuring outstanding service and results. For example, when a friend of mine went shopping for her wedding dress, most of the stores asked questions like, "What styles do you like?" Her answer was always the same—"Nothing poufy." She tried on dozens of dresses that matched that description but didn't quite meet her need. However, at the third store she visited, the saleswoman instead asked her, "How have you always dreamt of looking on your big day?" My friend lit up and chatted for several minutes about the venue, the decorations, and how she dreamt of looking "timeless and elegant." After their conversation, the saleswoman brought her THE dress! The whole shopping experience was changed by a question that differentiated this store from the rest.

Consider an upcoming customer interaction.
LIST THREE HIGH-LEVEL QUESTIONS
you can ask to uncover and understand their needs.

Even if you or your service providers aren't in an industry where you can spend a lot of time asking quality questions of each customer, when you ask a question, you must actively listen to the answer.

Asking questions is one way to anticipate and meet customer needs. But the most important part of the interaction is listening. Not all listening is created equal. Sometimes we appear as though we are listening—we're looking at the speaker; we may appear attentive—but we might not be taking in what's being said. To gain a clear understanding of needs and to create memorable moments, we need to devote our full attention to the customer and make sure they know we're paying close attention to everything they say. Active listening is more than hearing what someone says, it's also understanding what the person means or feels. Let me share an example.

I have a friend who *hates* to go shopping and only goes when she absolutely has to. One such instance was when she was searching for a new job and needed a new suit for her interviews. She walked into the first store and felt immediately overwhelmed, not knowing where to even start. Eventually, she approached a salesperson. "I'm not very good at this," she said. "Could you help me find a nice suit?" The salesperson pointed her in the right direction but didn't go any further than that. Unsure of what she was looking for, my friend left the store. She went to the second store, disgruntled and ready to give up. Immediately, a salesperson sensed her frustration and approached her to ask how she could help. When my friend explained again that she finds shopping difficult but needed new interview clothes, the employee got right to work. She pulled a variety of sizes, colors, and styles, and worked with my friend until they found what was right. The employees at the first store heard her say that she needed a suit but didn't listen to what she really needed—support and guidance. At the second store, they took note of her feelings and frustrations and actively listened to the need behind the need.

Tips for
ACTIVE LISTENING:

- **Pay attention to your client's tone of voice** and respond appropriately.

- **Use open body language** to show you are sincerely interested.

- **Confirm and summarize** what you hear.

- **Don't assume anything.**

- **Dig and listen.**

Ultimately, the only thing that really matters in a Platinum Service encounter is the customer's perception of what occurred. When you are intentional about talking WITH people, not TO them, then you show you care.

The following **four Ps** will give an additional and easy way to stay ahead of your customer's needs:

1. PEOPLE:

You have to ask questions. Pay attention. Actively listen. Read their body language. Make a mental note. What did the person say? What expression was on their face? What did they say without using words?

2. PRODUCT:

What problem does your product or service solve? What solution does your product provide to the end-user? Does everyone who needs to know about it "get it" and hear about it on a daily basis? How can you leverage what you know about the unique qualities of your product or service to anticipate your customer's unspoken needs?

3. PROCESS:

A customer relationship management database (CRM) holds customer information to learn what customers like, dislike, and how they use a specific platform. Instagram, Facebook, Snapchat, and Netflix all have CRMs and algorithms that customize the platform to their customers. Instagram and Facebook track who their customers follow, and what they like, to target specific products and companies in advertisements on their customers' feed. For example, someone who follows makeup brands and posts pictures tagging the products they use will have targeted marketing to mirror their interests. Just like how an employee at your favorite coffee shop may suggest another item based off of your order, CRMs do the same thing.

4. PRICE:

If you're simply pushing a product or service, then you'll have to compete on price. But if you can demonstrate your added value, then price isn't as important. For example, I pay about $11.50 for a burger and fries at Five Guys Burgers and Fries, a treat I give myself four times a year. Compare that to the $6 or $7 burgers at other fast-food restaurants. Why do I pay more for Five Guys? Maybe it's the barrels of free peanuts they give while I wait. And it's definitely that extra scoop of fries that gets me every time. They anticipate my needs and offer more than the competition. For that, I will pay more.

DON'T WAIT
for your customers to tell you what they want.
By then it may be too late!

Platinum Service means that you anticipate and uncover their needs—then deliver the service—before they even realize they need it. This proactive approach will leave a permanent imprint on the heart and mind of every customer. Commit to exceeding expectations and make it standard operating procedure. Welcome to your new way of life!

CHAPTER

RESPOND
With **Immediate** and **Appropriate Service**

FIVE

When I was with Disney, the company was relentless about what it called "guest recovery," which meant that if a cast member (employee)—whether on or off official duty—witnessed an incident that would dissatisfy a guest or would put a damper on their experience, we were to act immediately to recover that experience. So, if a four-year-old child dropped his ice cream cone seconds after taking his first lick, we quickly ran to buy him another one. We wouldn't let that family's magical moment be disrupted any longer than necessary.

Likewise, at the Disney resorts, it's not uncommon for a cast member to run to a nearby store if a guest merely mentions that they forgot a certain item at home. It was never too much trouble to recover the experience of a guest. We were taught to deliver Platinum Service without regard for inconvenience or nominal cost. We always looked through the lens of the guest, not ourselves.

It's never too much trouble to **RECOVER** the
EXPERIENCE
of a guest.

Responding with immediate and appropriate service is about seizing each moment to go above and beyond to fulfill a need.

I've been with the same service provider since I first purchased a cell phone. I love smartphones and have upgraded when they have something new on the market. In fact, my cell phone plan is so old that they've grandfathered all my cool benefits from the old plan into the new one. Totally awesome, right? Well, almost. That is, until I lost my phone.

According to The Conference Board, which recently surveyed 1,000 CEOs, presidents, and chairmen, marketing can sell the dream, but customer service can deliver a nightmare. The No. 1 thing that keeps these leaders up at night is human capital development. No. 2 is customer relationships. Are you surprised? I'm not.

While traveling from Washington, D.C., to San Francisco, somewhere between my hotel and the airport, my phone went missing. It was truly a fingernails-on-the-chalkboard moment. I cringed and thought to myself, *"What in the H-E-double-hockey-sticks happened to my phone?"* I'd never lost my phone in broad daylight before. When I got to the airport, I feverishly looked for a pay phone and found one near the Delta Air Lines TSA line.

First, I called my provider, and they told me that I could suspend my service temporarily. Second, my phone was turned off, which meant that I couldn't use the Find My iPhone app to locate it. I told my provider that my phone was insured, and they transferred me to a third-party company that handles their insurance claims. Here's where the wheels fell off the wagon, and why non-responsive service will kill your business.

SPARK
SNUFFER NO. 1:

BEFORE THE PROBLEM IS SOLVED,
don't ask the customer to TAKE A SURVEY.

Marketing is forever being judged by metrics, and I totally get that. But would you believe that as they were transferring me over to the third-party company—which shall remain nameless for now—they put a supervisor on the phone to see if I had a good experience? I'm not making this up. And then to add insult to injury, they asked me if I were to take a survey, would I recommend their service? Well, let's see. You've jammed me up in a corner, testing my love for your brand, so I guess the answer is "yes" for now.

They should've asked what they could do to be sure the issue was resolved, not if I'd take some bonehead survey so they could meet their key performance indicators and service goals. Get things in the correct order; solve the problem and then ask for feedback.

SNUFFER NO. 2:

ESTABLISHED SERVICE STANDARDS aren't
COMMUNICATED INTERNALLY
or to third-party partners.

After telling my story once again, the new representative said that my phone would be shipped out in one to two business days. Perfect, I thought. I was heading to San Francisco and would be re-united with my second wife—my smartphone—when I arrived. Two days later, I'm in San Francisco, but I had no smartphone and no way to explain what had happened. I felt like the guy who asks a girl to dance and she says to wait right where you are and never comes back.

Next, I was flying to Dallas from San Francisco. I called the company when I got to Dallas and asked what happened. The representative started going through a dissertation about how the warehouse ran out of phones and my order was not processed. I asked for his manager and suggested that I could go to the local retail store in Dallas and pick up a replacement. All he had to do was put it in the system and handle it on his end. He said, "No. We don't operate that way."

He should've given me several options instead of being another roadblock. He should also have offered to provide me a temporary phone while my new one was in transit. Instead, I believed he wanted to get me off the phone as fast as possible. A Platinum Service response requires a company and its people to be accountable. Taking ownership of a branded moment is about taking full responsibility for your actions and the customer's needs. This clearly was NOT an immediate or appropriate response!

SPARK
SNUFFER NO. 3:

Don't forget to
KEEP THE CUSTOMER
IN THE LOOP.

The guy said that he'd put the order in again himself and that I'd have my phone in one to two days. Okay, great. I arrived at my next city, Detroit, and still no phone. By this time, it was a week later, and I was phoneless in Detroit. Another key Platinum Service response quality is to be proactive. A sure way to show eagerness in responding to customers is to drop everything. Be available, visible, and willing to step in. Well, I was on an unplanned digital vacation and not feeling the love.

I called my cell provider from a landline and a young lady named Penny answered the phone. She empathized with my pain, then told me that she'd have to transfer me back over to their third-party company. She couldn't do anything for me, but she said I'd receive a survey where I could give feedback about how she'd handled my call. I realized that she was only doing her job and totally didn't get it.

Meanwhile, her company spends hundreds of millions of dollars for celebrity endorsements who tout their superior service. But the truth is that they can't take care of a fifteen-year loyal customer. I've always paid my bills, and over the years I've added two more cell numbers for my children. I am committed to them, but I question if they are committed to me. Why? They never emailed me or called my alternate phone number with an update. They left me in the dark. As you can imagine, this whole experience left a bad taste in my mouth, and I'm looking into other providers.

Research tells us that Americans, on average, tell nine people about good customer service experiences, but...they tell an average of sixteen people (nearly two times more) about bad service experiences—and that's BEFORE they get on any form of social media! Also, according to a survey conducted by American Express, 78 percent of consumers have cancelled or not made an intended purchase due to poor customer service. Other studies have shown that it takes several positive customer experiences to make up for one negative one. And that's not all. According to another reliable source, The Wharton School of Business at the University of Pennsylvania, for every 100 target customers, 64 percent will have heard about a business's poor service. And no matter what that business does to attract customers—such as discounts and advertising—that 64 percent will never buy at that business. Let's face it—people talk. You can't afford to let customer complaints cost you your SPARK.

If you can't fulfill your promise to your customers, then let them know right away and reset their expectations. Whatever you did to market your way into their heart, you have to do the same to keep them loyal to you.

If you can't **FULFILL YOUR PROMISE TO YOUR CUSTOMERS,** then let them know right away and **RESET THEIR EXPECTATIONS.** Whatever you did to market your way into their heart, you have to do the same to keep them loyal to you.

Let's look at a contrasting example. Delta Air Lines continues to get it right when it comes to responding with immediate and appropriate service. Being responsive requires being flexible. By this I mean having the willingness to "flex" your actions and processes in order to respond to customer needs and circumstances in the most effective way. Delta recently eliminated their check-in process to speed up the time it takes for users to check in. It's a detail that will make it quicker and more convenient for travelers to get where they're going. Despite the fact that many people can already check-in online, Delta is going the extra inch to deliver Platinum Service.

Let me explain. I was traveling to Palm Springs and Los Angeles with my two young adult children for a week-long vacation. It was going to be our last trip for a while since they were graduating from high school, driving, starting jobs, going to college, and shifting into less dependence on me and their mother. It was very important to me that the experience be perfect for them.

Our last meal was at Jean-Georges, an exquisite restaurant located in the Waldorf Astoria in Beverly Hills. We were floating on a cloud of magical memories as our trip was coming to an end. How could this amazing time with my two favorite people in the entire world get any better?

Imagine my surprise when we checked into Delta Air Lines Sky Priority lane at Los Angeles International airport (LAX) for our return flight to Orlando and found that both my daughter and I were upgraded to first class for our five-hour cross-country trip back to Orlando, Florida.

But as the last group of passengers were boarding, the gate agent pulled us aside and said that we'd have to give up our first-class seats and move back to seats 26 A & C. This was the last leg of our trip, and we were both quite disappointed. We felt that something we'd gained was now lost. And it was.

This may seem like a small issue, but the devil is in the details. Moments like this can make or break a customer's experience. Going the extra inch beyond the extra mile is what creates customer love and delivers Platinum Service. In situations like this, it's the recovery that counts.

Justin Simmons, the lead Delta Air Lines agent, understood this. He came back to apologize to us for what happened and said that when he closed out the upgrades, he neglected to notice that two first-class seats had been purchased at the last minute.

I understood what happened. However, a lot of people take situations like this and pour their pain out on social media or Yelp, just so they feel heard. It was important to me that Justin took the time to acknowledge our disappointment and mitigate any hard feelings. Justin demonstrated a key quality of a Platinum Service recovery. He empathized. When you empathize with the customer, you put yourself in their shoes.   A disappointed customer might just want you to demonstrate your concern. We're not talking about sympathy here; we're not saying you should "feel sorry" for the customer. Just listen patiently.

To recover a disappointing moment:

1. **Acknowledge that the experience was indeed negative.**

2. **Express that you are personally regretful that the customer is disappointed.**

3. **Be sincere and careful to use language that blames someone.**

Further, when I called the Delta SkyMiles Diamond Medallion Member representative and explained what had happened, the agent immediately apologized and deposited 10,000 miles into my account and 10,000 miles into my daughter's account. Now that's Platinum Service! One sure way to go above and beyond in a service recovery situation is to encourage the customer to vent.

In small business, for every customer who actually complains, twenty-six other customers decide to keep their complaints to themselves. That might sound like good news, because it's six to seven times more expensive to acquire a new customer than to keep a current one. However, to improve, you NEED to hear from customers and know where the problems lie in ensuring 100 percent satisfaction.

Hear the customer out and suspend judgment. As difficult as that might be, sometimes just listening—letting that disappointed customer unload—solves the problem. An important point to remember when it comes to taking ownership is that it may not be your fault, but it is your problem! Act on behalf of your company. And how many times, when you've been faced with an upset customer, did they end up thanking you or even apologizing at the end of the conversation?!

DON'T BE A STATISTIC!
Give your customers the respect they deserve
by acknowledging—and addressing—their problems immediately.

Here's what my Delta experience taught me about delivering Platinum Service:

- **It's all about the recovery.** Although Delta Air Lines couldn't undo the mistake, they recovered by gifting some airline miles into our accounts. We felt like we'd gained something despite our initial loss, and Delta was now assured that we'd fly with them again using those miles. This would give us another chance to experience their service.

- **If you hear it, you own it.** Once Justin heard about the hiccup, he took ownership of the experience. He could have passed the buck or let us continue without acknowledging what had happened. After all, we didn't purchase the first-class seats. Since they were given to us, it would have been easy to minimize—or even ignore—our disappointment.

- **Customer service isn't a department, it's a mindset.** Justin didn't work in the customer service department, but he made sure to discuss the event with us to acknowledge us and make us feel like our experience mattered. And the Sky-Miles Diamond rep didn't transfer us to another customer service department. They righted the wrong right then and there.

Customer service
isn't a department,
IT'S A MINDSET.

On the other end of the recovery continuum is the prospect of being a hero. The mark of a hero is the unexpected actions that, although not required of them, solve a problem in a way that surprises and redeems the service breakdown. A hero also shows kindness while performing their valiant acts. Being a customer recovery hero implies action AND empathy.

A Carey School of Business at Arizona State University study found that only 37 percent of customers were satisfied with service recovery when offered compensation in the form of monetary value, such as a refund or credit. However, when the company added an apology on top of the reparation, the customer satisfaction with the resolution increased to 74 percent. A service hero can make all the difference in whether a customer will return after a negative experience.

When a customer experiences an issue, they shouldn't have to ask for something to make it right. A hero surprises them with an extra step that not only fixes the situation but does so in a way that brands the moment. If an employee missteps, there is an open opportunity to rewrite the narrative for the customer. Make sure your people roll out the red carpet so that the customer believes they have gained something after their loss or inconvenience. Instead of simply turning lemons into lemonade, serve the customer a glass full of freshly squeezed lemonade in an elegant glass with a fancy straw, an umbrella garnish, and serve it ice-cold with a warm smile.

Respond to a customer need by
doing something
EXTRAORDINARY.

HERE ARE
6 WAYS TO SPARK
a VICTORIOUS RESPONSE:

1. KNOW THE ANSWERS OR HOW TO FIND THEM.

Research shows that 78 percent of customers say they expect to be able to find the correct solution for their problem by using self-service means. But when they DO call, whoever they speak to fails to answer their questions about 50 percent of the time, according to small-business consumers. It's critical to know your information. For example, in the restaurant business, wait staff need to be able to answer questions regarding ingredients and how food is prepared. If a customer asks, "Is there gluten in this? I'm allergic," the waiter needs to be able to confidently respond in the moment, and assure them their food is safe to eat.

2. GIVE "INSIDE INFORMATION."

Customers like to believe they are getting special treatment and firsthand tips on a particular need. In some cases, travel agencies will choose to display their competitors' rates, even when theirs isn't the best deal, in an effort to build trust with their customers. Customers who have been scammed or ripped off by other booking websites may see value in this and choose the higher rate. Perhaps you can put a price on trust.

3. OFFER ALTERNATIVES.

If you don't have exactly what the customer is asking for, offer options and explain the value. Three out of five Americans say they'd try something new or different if it meant a better customer service experience. A friend of mine arrived late in the evening to a hotel with his family. They had just spent the entire day traveling and were quite tired and hungry. Unfortunately, the hotel restaurant had just closed. Noticing their defeated expressions, the concierge told them to drop off their luggage in their room and then proceed back to the lobby and she would have a plan for them. While they were dropping off their bags, the concierge quickly researched a comparable restaurant, called ahead to reserve a table, and had a cab ready to go as soon as the family returned to the lobby. My friend and his family may not have spent their money at the hotel's establishment, but because of that service, they returned to the hotel for future stays.

4. SOLVE A PROBLEM.

Any time you solve a customer's challenge, big or small, you have a chance to be a hero. Seventy percent of the time, if you can solve a problem—or resolve a complaint in the customer's favor—they will do business with you again. When I stayed at the Langham Hotel in Chicago, I got up early to workout one morning. The gym wasn't open yet, so I sought out a security guard who would understand my plight to tone up my wannabe six pack. It was 5:45 a.m. on a Saturday morning and this fellow was full of energy and excited about his job. He asked me to follow him and took me to the back of the hotel. I noticed a piece of flip-chart paper posted to the back of the door where employees would see it before they walked out to the public area. The poster was entitled "Chasing Consistency" with a list of behaviors that were expected by every employee before they entered the public space. When I asked him about it, he said, "In order for us to be No. 1, we have to chase consistency." Well, he let me in. He solved my problem. Being the doubting Thomas that I can be at times, I thought to myself, "Calm down; it's not that deep." I went to workout and returned to my room within an hour. I went online to TripAdvisor.com to see what the fuss about the Langham Hotel Chicago was all about. Well, indeed, they were ranked No.1 out of 184 hotels in the Chicagoland market. However, that was 2013. I checked again in 2017 and once again, the Langham Hotel Chicago was still No. 1. That's when it clicked. Chasing consistency was in the DNA of their culture. They do the little things right by responding immediately and appropriately—and going the extra inch.

5. **GO OUT OF YOUR WAY TO ACCOMMODATE A REQUEST.**

REACH HIGHER!
They EXPECT YOU TO.

Eighty percent of Americans believe smaller companies place more emphasis on customer service than their larger counterparts. Remember my Nordstrom's experience? I've never seen an organization respond in such an immediate and appropriate way! They executed Platinum Service immediately. When I arrived, clothes were already in the dressing room and a tailor was standing by. And Armann, my retail expert, went the extra inch by providing lotion and cologne testers.

6. SHOW THE CUSTOMER YOU VALUE THEIR TIME.

Perhaps one of the most heroic things you can do when responding to a customer need is to let them see you value their time. Next to feeling poorly treated, a top reason customers leave a brand is their failure to resolve a customer's problem in a timely manner. Think about my phone carrier experience!

• • •

In some of the research we've been referring to, we found that 41 percent of small business consumers expect a customer service email response within six hours...but only 36 percent of companies actually responded to service emails that quickly. Another study found that small business consumers said 24 hours is widely considered an "acceptable email response time." In either case, let the customer see you value their time.

Let's put this all together. Imagine you are a customer in this scenario. You're at a local hamburger joint. You order a burger well-done. No cheese. Extra pickles. The server brings back the burger. Extra pickles. No cheese. But, when you cut the burger open, it is practically raw. Definitely not well-done, more like rare. You tilt the burger toward the server, whose eyes open wide in realization that the burger is undeniably not cooked properly. The server immediately apologizes understandingly, and scoops up the plate to have the kitchen remake it. The server brings back the side of fries so that you have something to munch on while the burger is being re-cooked.

A few minutes later, the server brings back the burger and guess what? Now, when you cut it in half, the burger is charred and black on the outside. The server gives another genuine apology and immediately goes to get the manager. The manager not only comps the meal, but surprises you with a slice of cheesecake on the house at the end of the meal.

Comping the meal would have been "enough" to fix the misstep. But the cheesecake at the end and the server's genuine understanding and apology were heroic.

Remember to serve the customer with the unexpected after the unexpected has occurred.

When you go the extra inch to respond with Platinum Service, you demonstrate your commitment to the customer and can win their love forever.

What can you do **TO DELIVER** PLATINUM **RESPONSES**
and be more...?

- Flexible

- Proactive

- Accountable

- Heroic

"

"In the world of
internet customer
service, it's important
to remember your
competitor is only
one mouse click away."

— Douglas Warner,
Board of Directors, General Electric

CHAPTER

KEEP
Them Loyal Through
Acts of Kindness

SIX

Do you know how valuable loyal customers are? For small businesses, loyal customers are worth up to ten times the amount they spend on their first purchase.

Not only is it expensive to acquire new customers, you've only got a 5% TO 20% PROBABILITY of SELLING TO A NEW PROSPECT.

On the other hand, the probability of selling to an existing customer is 60 percent to 70 percent.

To keep customers happy, loyal, and purchasing again, you must surprise and delight them. Deliver your Platinum Service in creative ways and they'll be back for more!

Most people love surprises, as long as they are pleasant. Not surprisingly, the study of the emotional reaction to a surprise—yes, there is such a thing—has its roots in psychology. There's a lot of clinical gobbledygook about it, but the *Journal of Emotional Psychology* says that surprise is an emotion elicited by something unexpected, and the impact of a surprise is measured by "excitation transfer."

Focus on
SURPRISING AND DELIGHTING YOUR CUSTOMERS,
which means going above and beyond to make each Platinum Service moment memorable and enjoyable.

Here's how it works:

- When a Platinum Service moment triggers a pleasant reaction, the level of joy will be even higher if the person is surprised.

- Because surprise amplifies emotions, customers who are pleasantly surprised will be more delighted, which will alter their behavior. In other words, they'll spend more, come back, or tell people about their positive experience, all of which creates customer loyalty.

Study after study has found that organizations that are leaders in their respective industries do more than just provide good service. Instead, they provide Platinum Service moments that surprise and delight their target customers in ways the customer values the most.

And the results of surprising and delighting customers are higher customer satisfaction scores, greater profit, and increased customer loyalty. Doing something a little extra is worth the investment. In fact, one study even showed that waiters receive a 21 percent better tip when they leave two mints. Small efforts yield big payoffs!

Perhaps the most obvious benchmark is Disney, a company whose core philosophy centers on hiring and training people who genuinely take pleasure in delighting guests.

My friend Mel Robbins has built a movement on the five-second rule. I remember that when I worked at Disney, they encouraged employees to "take 5," or spend five seconds to make a memory. They called these "Magic Moments." You may have heard some of the stories:

- Cast members give commemorative pins to children who are celebrating birthdays.

- A groundskeeper invites a senior guest who'd been intently watching them turn a flower bed to "help."

- Characters spend extra time with children in wheelchairs.

- Custodial hosts offer to take a photo of two guests when they notice that one of them is taking a picture of the other.

When Southwest Airlines finds out that guests are on their honeymoon, they often surprise them by making a congratulatory announcement and gifting them a bottle of champagne.

Many healthcare providers know the value of surprise as well. For example, one of our colleagues purchased two pairs of glasses from a new doctor's office. Six months later his prescription changed quite dramatically. Understanding the patient's disappointment, the store where they purchased their glasses replaced the lenses in both frames, free of charge.

• • •

To keep your customers coming back, why not AMAZE THEM?!

In previous SPARK chapters, we've looked at some of these approaches, such as acknowledging customers to make a positive impression, making a connection, and adding a special touch to personalize the service. Think of AMAZE as the tool that brings it all together.

Here are eight ways to truly
AMAZE YOUR CUSTOMERS:

1. ACKNOWLEDGE THEM IMMEDIATELY.

When we put on our customer hat, we leave our patient shoes in the car. As a customer, the last thing we want is to wait in a long line to spend our money. Apple has a unique way of handling large crowds. Rather than having you wait around frustrated, they greet you right away and get you checked in. From there you're free to roam about the store until they have a moment to assist you. They also take this a step further. They don't just call your name, they find you in the crowd and come directly to you, greeting you and introducing themselves.

2. MAKE A MEMORABLE CONNECTION.

Use every opportunity you can to show your customers who you are and what they mean to you. Especially in a digital age, ensure you connect with the human on the other end of every interaction. Phone representatives at the catalog company New Pig sell all kinds of absorbent mats and pads, and they do something small but special. They keep an assortment of greeting cards on a shelf in the order department. When a customer mentions a birthday or a noteworthy occasion, they simply reach for a card to commemorate the event, fill it out on the spot, and out it goes in the day's mail! This connection not only amazes, it keeps the customer loyal.

3. ADD A SPECIAL TOUCH.

As we've said before, delivering Platinum Service goes beyond doing only what is expected. It's important to make the customer feel special and valued. Whenever I go to Bonefish Grill restaurant—which, if I'm lucky, is once every six or nine months—a server named Sue greets me by name. And when I receive my bill, there's always a little handwritten thank-you on it. Wow, what a brilliant touch! That makes me want to push my tip over the 20 percent mark. When a colleague of mine was shopping for a house in a new area, his mortgage lender put together a personalized packet of information about local clubs, associations, or activities like golf or tennis, recognizing these were personal needs and preferences he had. The lender amazed my friend by listening to him and anticipating needs. Sometimes it comes down to doing something small but special to make a customer feel important. These personalized special touches make service memorable, and keep your customers coming back.

4. ZERO IN ON THEIR EMOTIONAL LEVEL.

Show them that you understand their feelings and needs beyond what is on the surface. To zero in on their emotional level, put yourself in your customer's shoes. If they pick up on the fact that you are empathetic to their situation, they'll appreciate it. To determine how they might be feeling, observe their body language and facial expressions. Listen not only to the words they say but also to their vocal tone. This will give an indication of what they are feeling or thinking. Once you observe how they're feeling, try to meet them at that level. Even if you do something as simple as offer to carry something for an overloaded customer, open a door, or entertain a child while a parent fills out paperwork, it can make a world of difference in how you and your company are perceived. The emotions will vary for every customer situation. That's why it's important to listen and watch for cues and clues to zero in on your customers' needs. When you meet them at their emotional level, it will surprise them and delight them.

5. END WITH A LASTING IMPRESSION.

Platinum Service closes by creating a memory. A lot of companies think that the beginning of an encounter is the most important to the customer, so they only focus on a friendly greeting. While a positive beginning is important, the closing is far more so. Forbes calls the closing a customer experience most businesses miss out on. Forbes says that a "memorable and sincere" service closing can ensure that a first impression doesn't go to waste. A colleague of mine observed a very special goodbye in a busy airport. A female employee was assisting a passenger traveling in a wheelchair. She apparently noted the passenger's emotional stress; the woman arrived at the gate in tears. The employee bent down and gave the passenger a hug. Was this a surprise? Indeed. Was this a Platinum moment for that airline? You bet. Will this leave a lasting impression on that customer? Of course it will.

Sometimes, it comes down to doing something small but special to make a customer feel important. This is really what makes Platinum Service memorable, and keeps your customers coming back.

Here are **THREE STEPS** that work every time to **CREATE A**
MEMORABLE IMPRESSION:

1. **Show sincere appreciation.**

2. **Invite them back.**

3. **Tailor the goodbye.**

The first two are obvious points, and they should never be over-looked. But to tailor the goodbye takes a little extra thought—and therein lies the surprise! We know from our friends at a convenience store that when a customer buys a lottery ticket, the employee will say, "good luck" or "let me know when you win." Many contact-center agents end with a simple "thanks for calling," and you've been to retailers who bid you "thanks for coming in."

Malaysia Airlines understands that a Platinum Service encounter isn't over when the customer steps off the plane. And their employees understand that. In fact, they had an older woman who was traveling with her infant son. It was a bit of a struggle for her, and she fondly remembers the help that the flight attendants gave her after they landed at their destination. They helped her at baggage claim and arranged her ground transportation. It cost the airline very little to provide that end-of-encounter assistance, and that loyal customer has told dozens of fellow travelers about her surprising and delightful experience.

Wait, there's more. After getting suited up that morning, I received an email from the Nordstrom Easton Town Center that said...

> "We hope to have you back in the store soon! Please don't hesitate to call us if you need anything."

Shhh …don't tell their competition to answer the phone or open early. We'll let them continue to sleep while Nordstrom shares the love.

"LOYAL CUSTOMERS COST LESS TO SERVE!
They pay more than other customers
and attract new customers through word of mouth!"*

These loud claims prompted one high-tech service provider to launch a $2 million-per-year customer-loyalty program. Five years later, the company made disturbing discoveries: Half of its loyal customers barely generated a profit, and half of its most profitable customers bought high-margin products once—then disappeared. What happened? According to an article in *Harvard Business Review,* the loyalty-equals-profitability equation is surprisingly weak—and complicated. Not all loyal customers are profitable, and not all profitable customers are loyal. Managing customers for loyalty doesn't automatically mean managing them for profits. To strengthen the loyalty-profitability link, you must manage both—simultaneously. Let's look at a few more ways to keep them coming back…

*(Source: "The Mismanagement of Customer Loyalty,"
by Werner Reinartz & V. Kumar - Harvard Business Review)

6. PRACTICE KINDNESS.

A sure way to surprise and delight is to sincerely flatter or praise. A small but genuine-sounding comment can go a long way. The key is to be sincere (not too over-the-top) and appropriate. So what kind of compliment could you give a customer, particularly if you don't know them personally? You could comment on an accessory they're wearing, such as a scarf, briefcase, or watch. If you're visiting their home or office, look for awards, photos, or other items that communicate pride or accomplishment. If your customer shares a story about a special talent, hobby, or achievement, be sure to show interest! Look for ways to demonstrate random acts of kindness. Here's a great example:

Sweetgreen is a restaurant destination for healthy, organic food sourced from trusted local farmers. It was formed on the core value of creating meaningful connections from farm to patron. This startup wants to align what you eat with what you value, so they strive to create meaningful relationships by giving back to their customers and the local community. More importantly, every employee is entrusted to be the face and hands of the restaurant. Employees from California to Virginia can be found doing "random acts of sweetness." You might catch sweetgreen teams handing out restaurant gift cards to recognize people who are doing good things for their communities. They've been spotted tucking gift cards onto vehicle windows to cover a parking ticket, saving the owner the downer of getting a ticket. And, if it's raining, you might find a shower cap on your bike seat with a gift certificate underneath! These types of actions trigger the desire to reciprocate and can earn that person's loyalty for a long time. And sweetgreen's sales figures back the value of that Platinum Service.

Their current revenue of $10 million to $15 million in sales represents a 300 percent year-over-year growth since their inception.

If you are a
HIRING MANAGER,
HIRE KIND PEOPLE.

If you are an employee, practice kindness. Whether you're grocery shopping or volunteering, look for ways to meet the needs of others. As I mentioned in the Personalize chapter (Chapter 3), companies must hire for attitude and train for success. Training can't fix what management doesn't catch during the interview process. After the hiring is done, embed the spirit of consistency and service excellence in your people. Recognize when their performance is spot on. Who people are is so much more important than what they can do at the moment. The most-admired companies in the world take hiring seriously. They look not only for a great attitude but one that fits their culture.

Tom Bohn at NAVC looks for just this. All NAVC candidates must go through three levels of screening and, regardless of level, the process culminates with an interview with Tom himself. His entire focus is on cultural fit. In his interview, he talks about things like work-life balance, sense of humor, passion for the work they will be doing, and what an ideal workplace looks like. All candidates fill out a questionnaire about purpose and their passion in life.

7. LET YOUR IMPACT LINGER.

Follow up, follow up, follow up. Nothing can ruin or solidify a Platinum Service moment quicker than thoughtful and thorough follow-up—or the lack thereof. It could be as simple as making a quick phone call to see if the customer is feeling better or to see how an important meeting went, or sending a handwritten thank-you note. There are a million and one ways to AMAZE, but you can't pass Go and Stop. Do you remember when you were first dating your spouse or significant other? You did whatever you had to do to capture their attention. If it meant fine dining, vintage wine, long walks in the park, and hours of conversation, you did it. But somewhere along the way, you may have stopped doing what caught their attention the first time. Ah—you may know where this is leading! Whatever you did to catch them, you have to do to keep them!

8. SURPRISE AND DELIGHT YOUR CUSTOMERS, AND YOU'LL KEEP THEM COMING BACK.

When it comes to delivering Platinum Service, you have to go beyond the first impression, and show your customers that they are truly valuable. Not only is retaining customers better for your bottom line, it also helps you differentiate yourself as a business that genuinely cares for the people it serves. Let your **SPARK** distinguish you from the pack through memorable, exceptional service that keeps them coming back—every time.

List three ideas to AMAZE customers in your business. How can you consistently end on a positive note?

"

"The level of our success
is limited only by our
imagination and no
act of kindness,
however small,
is ever wasted."

— Aesop

CONCLUS

I O N

Many years ago at Disney, Al Weiss, president, told me I need-ed to know *who I was* and *why I was really here*. Your organization and its people can't deliver Platinum Service until you can answer those two questions. You were created to find your purpose. A *job* is what you're paid to do; your *purpose* is what you are made to do. When you find your meaningful calling, your internal **SPARK** will ig-nite, placing you in the optimal position to deliver Platinum Service in your business.

That's right. I'm telling you that it's time to light the fire in your belly—to kindle your fire and passion. In today's competitive business world, there's no place for lackluster performance, half-brilliant con-tributions, or low-burning customer service.

IT'S TIME TO BECOME the
DOMINANT FORCE
in your life's work.

TODAY'S ECONOMY is weeding out bad attitudes, lackluster performance, and half-brilliant contributions.

Be the SPARK that creates the change you want to see in the world. Whatever space you consume, let it be filled with fire, passion, and energy that you intentionally exude. Let every person in your realm feel that energy, benefit from your passion, and remember how remarkable you made them feel.

YOUR
SPARK
STORY
BEGINS HERE.

SPARK

FIVE PLATINUM SERVICE PRINCIPLES
for Creating Customers for Life

S
SEE
them as guests

CUSTOMERS

CULTURE

CONNECTION

K
KEEP
them loyal through
acts of kindness

P
PERSONALIZE
the experience for
those you touch

LEADERS
The Platinum
Service Nucleus

CONNECTION

CULTURE

R
RESPOND
with immediate and
appropriate service

CUSTOMERS

A
ANTICIPATE
and uncover needs

BIBLIOGRAPHY

Introduction

1. G. Scott, Thomas. "Buffalo Named Third-Poorest City in U.S." Buffalo Business First, 29 Sep. 2009, bizjournals.com/buffalo/stories/2009/09/28/daily18.html. Accessed 23 June 2018.

2. "Netflix- Media Center." Netflix, 11 May 2018, www.media.netflix.com/en/about-netflix.

3. "Netflix- Quarterly Earnings." Netflix, June 2016, www.ir.netflix.com/quarterly-earnings.

4. "Netflix- Annual Reports & Proxies." Netflix, June 2016, www.ir.netflix.com/annual-reports.

CHAPTER 1: PLATINUM SERVICE Starts with Leaders

1. "2018 Best Places to Work – Employees' Choice." Glassdoor, www.glassdoor.com/Award/Best-Places-to-Work-LST_KQ0,19.htm.

2. "Top CEOs 2018 – Employees' Choice." Glassdoor, www.glassdoor.com/Award/Top-CEOs-LST_KQ0,8.htm.

3. "Undercover Boss." Television Academy Emmys, 2016, www.emmys.com/shows/undercover-boss.

4. "Culture." Merriam Webster, www.merriam-webster.com/dictionary/culture?src=search-dict-box.

5. Harvard Business Review. "The Culture Factor." Harvard Business Review, pro no. BR1801-MAG-ENG, 1 Jan. 2018, www.hbr.org/product/harvard-business-review-januaryfebruary-2018/BR1801-MAG-ENG.

6. North American Veterinary Community, PHOS Creative. NAVC Your Veterinary Community. North American Veterinary Community, 2018, https://navc.com/.

7. Kaytie Zimmerman. "5 Things We Know Millennials Want from a Job." Forbes, 1 Oct. 2017, www.forbes.com/sites/kaytiezimmerman/2017/10/01/5-things-we-know-Millennials-want-from-a-job/2/.

8. Fleming, John H. Harter, James K. "The Next Discipline- Applying Behavioral Economics to Drive Growth and Profitability." Gallup, 2009-2013, file:///C:/Users/cortn/AppData/Local/Packages/Microsoft.MicrosoftEdge_8wekyb3d8bbwe/TempState/Downloads/The%20Next%20Discipline%20-%20Applied%20Behavioral%20Economics%20(1).pdf

9. "Olive Garden." Student Series, http://www.studentseries.org/about/who-we-are/olive-garden.

10. "Olive Garden Partners With Boys & Girls Clubs for "Round Up 4 BGCA" Campaign." Wakebgc.org, 18 Sept. 2014, www.wakebgc.org/olive-garden-partners-with-boys-girls-clubs-for-round-up-for-bgca-campaign/.

11. Goalcast. "25 Maya Angelou Quotes to Inspire Your Life." Goalcast, 3 Apr.2017, www.goalcast.com/2017/04/03/maya-angelou-quotes-to-inspire-your-life/.

12. Gates, Lisa. "Coaching and Developing Employees." LinkedIn.com, 11 May 2013, www.linkedin.com/learning/coaching-and-developing-employees/welcome.

13. "Global Digital Population as of April 2018 (in millions)." Statista.com, Apr. 2018, www.statista.com/statistics/617136/digital-population-worldwide/.

14. "MetLife's 9th Annual Study of Employee Benefits Trends." Benefit Administration Group, 31 Mar. 2011, www.bagllc.com/blog/metlifes-9th-annual-study-of-employee-benefits-trends/.

15. Garson. "The Place Where Your Talent Meets the World's Needs Is the Job God Has in Mind for You." Quote Investigator, 20 Dec. 2017, www.quoteinvestigator.com/2017/12/20/talent/.

CHAPTER 2: S= SEE Them as Guests

1. "The Top 10 Reasons You Don't Understand Your Customers." Bain & Company, 1 May 2006, www.bain.com/publications/articles/top-10-reasons-you-dont-understand-your-customers.aspx.

2. https://www.lindsayelizabeth.com/.

3. "Culture of CARE." Provision Healthcare, 2018, www. provisionhealthcare.com/patient-care/culture-of-care/.

4. Carey, Shannon. "Victory Bell Rings at Provision." www. provisionhealthcare.com/wp-content/uploads/2017/05/Bearden_ Shopper-News_030314.pdf.

5. "About Thomas M. Bohn, CAE." NAVC, 2018, www.navc.com/staff/ thomas-m-bohn-cae/.

6. Pulido, Alfonso. Stone, Dorian. Strevel, John. "The Three Cs of Customer Satisfaction: Consistency, Consistency, Consistency." McKinsey, Mar. 2014, www.mckinsey.com/industries/retail/ our-insights/the-three-cs-of-customer-satisfaction-consistency- consistency-consistency.

7. "45 Small Business Customer Service Statistics That Justify a Strategy Shift." Conversational Receptionists, 10 Jun. 2016, www.conversational.com/45-small-business-customer-service- statistics-justify-strategy-shift/.

8. Carnegie, Dale. How to Win Friends and Influence People, Simon & Schuster, 1936.

9. "Net Promoter Score Calculation." Survey Monkey, 1999-2018, www.surveymonkey.com/mp/net-promoter-score-calculation/.

10. "Net Promoter Driving Loyalty in Lean Times." Satmetrix, 9 Jun. 2009, www.icbe.ie/Documents/Symp2011_Satmetrix.pdf.

CHAPTER 3: P = PERSONALIZE the Experience

1. "45 Important Small Business Customer Service Statistics." Conversational Receptionist, 10 Jun. 2016, www.conversational. com/45-small-business-customer-service-statistics-justify- strategy-shift/.

2. "Cardinal Health Completes Acquisition of the Harvard Drug Group For $1.115 Billion." Cardinal Health, 6 Jul. 2015, www. ir.cardinalhealth.com/news/press-release-details/2015/Cardinal- Health-Completes-Acquisition-of-the-Harvard-Drug-Group-for- 1115-Billion/default.aspx. 2018

3. Belludi, Nagesh, "Albert Mehrabian's 7-38-55 Rule of Personal Communication." Right Attitudes, 4 Oct. 2008, www.rightattitudes.com/2008/10/04/7-38-55-rule-personal-communication/.

4. Taylor, Mike. "10 Powerfully Persuasive Words Your Customers Want to Hear." Entrepreneur, 2 Aug. 2016, https://www.entrepreneur.com/article/279224.

5. Burke, Kenneth. "How Many Texts Do People Send Every Day?" Textrequest, 18 May 2016, https://www.textrequest.com/blog/how-many-texts-people-send-per-day/.

6. "Internet Usage in the United States – Statistics & Facts." Statistica, 2016.

7. "Twitter Usage Statistics." Internet Live Stats, 28 Jun. 2018, http://www.internetlivestats.com/twitter-statistics/.

8. Crystal, David. The Stories of English. London, United Kingdom, Penguin Books Ltd, 01, Jan. 2006.

9. Ekstein, Nikki. "Why Little Alaska Airlines Has the Happiest Customers in the Sky." Bloomberg, 24, May 2017, https://www.bloomberg.com/news/articles/2017-05-24/how-alaska-airlines-became-the-best-airline-in-the-u-s.

10. Big Cartel. Easy Online Stores for Artists & Makers, 2005, https://www.bigcartel.com/.

11. "Consumers Want Conversational Virtual Assistants." Nuance, 13, Mar. 2015, https://www.nuance.com/content/dam/nuance/en_uk/collateral/enterprise/white-paper/wp-consumers-want-conversational-virtual-assistants-en-us.pdf.

12. Chewy. Pet Food, Products, Supplies at Low Prices, 2011, www.chewy.com.

CHAPTER 4: A = ANTICIPATE and Uncover Needs

1. "45 Small Business Customer Service Statistics That Justify a Strategy Shift." Conversational Receptionists, 10 Jun. 2016, www.conversational.com/45-small-business-customer-service-statistics-justify-strategy-shift/.

2. Hainla, Liis. "21 Social Media Marketing Statistics You Need to Know in 2018." Dreamgrow, 25, Jun. 2018, https://www.

dreamgrow.com/21-social-media-marketing-statistics/.

3.   Osman, Maddy. "28 Powerful Facebook Stats Your Brand Can't Ignore in 2018." Sproutsocial, 15 Feb. 2018, www.sproutsocial. com/insights/facebook-stats-for-marketers/.

4.   Standberry, Sherman. "The Ultimate List: 75 Benefits of Social Media Marketing." Lyfemarketing, 28, May 2015, www. lyfemarketing.com/roi-benefits-social-media-marketing/.

5.   Clifford, Stephanie. "Video Prank at Domino's Taints Brand." The New York Times, 15, Apr. 2009, https://www.nytimes. com/2009/04/16/business/media/16dominos.html.

6.   White, Jeremy. "2011 Pizza Chain of the Year – Domino's Pizza." Pizza Today, 1 Jun. 2011, https://www.pizzatoday.com/ departments/features/2011-june-chain-of-the-year/.

CHAPTER 5: R = RESPOND with Immediate and Appropriate Service

1.   The Conference Board, 5 May. 2016, www.conference-board.org/.

2.   Markidan, Len. "22 Customer Support Statistics That You Absolutely Need to Know." Groovehq, 14 Feb. 2017, www. groovehq.com/support/customer-support-statistics.

3.   "Good Service is Good Business: American Customers Willing to Spend More With Companies That Get Service Right, According to American Express Survey." American Express, 3 May 2011, www.about.americanexpress.com/news/pr/2011/csbar.aspx.

4.   Thornton, Kendall. "18 Interesting Stats to Get You Rethinking Your Customer Service Process." Salesforce, 14 Aug. 2013, www. salesforce.com/blog/2013/08/customer-service-stats.html.

5.   "Beware of Dissatisfied Consumers: They Like to Blab." Wharton School of Business, 8 Mar. 2006, www.knowledge.wharton.upenn. edu/article/beware-of-dissatisfied-consumers-they-like-to-blab/.

6.   "45 Small Business Customer Service Statistics That Justify a Strategy Shift." Conversational Receptionists, 10 Jun. 2016, www.conversational.com/45-small-business-customer-service-statistics-justify-strategy-shift/.

7.   W.P. Carey School of Business at Arizona State University. "Holiday Spirit Turns to Rage when Customers Need Service." Prnewswire, 2 Dec. 2015, www.prnewswire.com/news-releases/holiday-spirit-

turns-to-rage-when-customers-need-service-300187353.html.

8. "45 Important Small Business Customer Service Statistics." Conversational Receptionists, 10 Jun. 2016. http://www. conversational.com/45-small-business-customer-service-statistics-justify-strategy-shift/.

9. "45 Important Small Business Customer Service Statistics." Conversational Receptionists, 10 Jun. 2016. http://www. conversational.com/45-small-business-customer-service-statistics-justify-strategy-shift/.

10. "45 Important Small Business Customer Service Statistics." Conversational Receptionists, 10 Jun. 2016. http://www. conversational.com/45-small-business-customer-service-statistics-justify-strategy-shift/.

11. "The Langham, Chicago." TripAdvisor, 2 Jul. 2018, www. tripadvisor.com/Hotel_Review-g35805-d4046139-Reviews-The_ Langham_Chicago-Chicago_Illinois.html.

12. "45 Small Business Customer Service Statistics That Justify a Strategy Shift." Conversational Receptionists, 10 Jun. 2016, www.conversational.com/45-small-business-customer-service-statistics-justify-strategy-shift/.

13. "45 Important Small Business Customer Service Statistics." Conversational Receptionists, 10 Jun. 2016. http://www. conversational.com/45-small-business-customer-service-statistics-justify-strategy-shift/.

14. "45 Important Small Business Customer Service Statistics." Conversational Receptionists, 10 Jun. 2016. http://www. conversational.com/45-small-business-customer-service-statistics-justify-strategy-shift/.

CHAPTER 6: K = KEEP Them Loyal through Acts of Kindness

1. Aksu, Hulya. "Customer Service: The New Proactive Marketing." Huffington Post, 26 Mar. 2013, www.huffingtonpost.com/hulya-aksu/customer-service-the-new-_b_2827889.html. Accessed 2 Jul. 2018.

2. "Journal of Emotional Psychology." American Psychological Association, 2018, www.psycnet.apa.org.

3. Ciotti, Gregory. "The Psychology of Personalization: How Restaurant Servers Increased Tips by 23 Percent (Without Changing Service)." HelpScout, 3 Apr. 2012, www.helpscout.net/blog/the-psychology-of-personalization-how-waiters-increased-tips-by-23-percent-without-changing-service/

4. New Pig – World's best products for leaks, drips, and spills. New Pig, 2018, www.newpig.com.

5. Solomon, Michah. "'You Had Me at Goodbye': The Customer Experience Expert Practice You're Probably Missing Out On." Forbes, 20 Mar. 2015, www.forbes.com/sites/micahsolomon/2015/03/20/have-your-customers-at-goodbye-a-customer-experience-expert-practice/#17e967666bf3.

6. Malaysia Airlines. Malaysia Aviation Group Corporate Structure, 19 May 2016, www.malaysiaairlines.com/us/en.html.

7. Reinartz, Werner. Kumar, V. "The Mismanagement of Customer Loyalty." Harvard Business Review, Jul. 2002, www.hbr.org/2002/07/the-mismanagement-of-customer-loyalty.

8. Rapkin, Mickey. "The Founders of sweetgreen are Building a Farm – to – Counter Empire, One Bowl at a Time." Fast Company, 21 Nov. 2016, www.fastcompany.com/3065372/the-founders-of-sweetgreen-are-building-a-farm-to-counter-empire-o.

9. "About Thomas M. Bohn, CAE." NAVC, 2018, www.navc.com/staff/thomas-m-bohn-cae/.

ABOUT THE AUTHOR

Simon T. Bailey is an Innovator, Educator, and Writer, whose life's purpose is to teach 1 billion+ people how to be fearless and create their future.

He has more than 30 years' experience in the hospitality industry, including serving as sales director for Disney Institute, and has worked with more than 1,600 organizations in 45 countries.

Simon has been named one of the top 25 people who will help you reach your business and life goals by SUCCESS magazine, joining a list that includes Brene Brown, Tony Robbins and Oprah Winfrey. He is the author of nine books, and his Building Business Relationships on Lynda.com has been viewed by more than 750,000 people. His Goalcast video, released Father's Day 2018, has over 57 million views as of this writing.

Simon holds a Master's degree from Faith Christian University and was inducted as an honorary member of the University of Central Florida Golden Key Honor Society.

When he is not working, Simon spends quality time with his two active teenagers, roots for the Buffalo Bills, and serves as a board member for U.S. Dream Academy, Orlando Health Foundation Board, and Florida Virtual School Foundation.

BOOKS & eBOOKS
by SIMON T. BAILEY

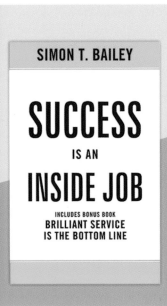
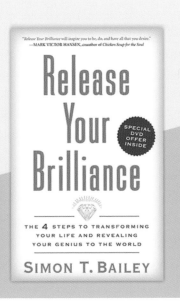

- *Simon Says Dream: Live a Passionate Life (out of print)*

- *Success is an Inside Job with bonus book Brilliant Service is the Bottom Line*

- *Release Your Brilliance: The 4 Steps to Transforming Your Life and Revealing Your Genius to the World (also available in Spanish and Portuguese)*

- *Shift Your Brilliance: Harness the Power of You, Inc.*

- *Brilliant Living: 31 Insights to Creating an Awesome Life*

- *Releasing Leadership Brilliance: Breaking Sound Barriers in Education co-written with Dr. Marceta F. Reilly*

- *Meditate on Your Personal Brilliance*

- *Meditate on Your Professional Brilliance*

SELF-PACED COURSES & TRAINING PROGRAMS

by **SIMON T. BAILEY**

SHIFT YOUR BRILLIANCE SYSTEM

Become your best self. Shift Your Brilliance helps you direct your own personal development narrative. You'll learn how to become a leader of the future and Chief Breakthrough Officer of your organization.

BRILLIANT PRESENTER

Everyone wants to be a speaker. Whether it's in the boardroom, to your family, or in front of 10,000 people, this course will teach you how to speak effectively. Give a brilliant presentation and watch the new clients, promotions, opportunities, and life changes start to roll in. Your life and career will be forever transformed.

SHIFT TO BRILLIANCE

This course will give you twelve ways to jumpstart your business, career, and life.

`00:01:34`

BUILDING BUSINESS RELATIONSHIPS

There are four key types of business relationships in your career: your manager, your coworkers, other departments, and executives. In this Lynda.com course, Simon is your guide to building authentic connections with others to create your own personal board of directors for success.

FINDING A SPONSOR

The workforce may be competitive, but you are not alone. The individuals who see your ambition and point you in the right direction can act as advocates. In this best-selling Lynda.com course, Simon helps you build a trusting relationship with a sponsor – and change the course of your career.

All books, eBooks, training programs, and courses
are available at www.simontbailey.com

CONNECT

with **SIMON T. BAILEY**

To Purchase "Be the SPARK" promotional products:

hello@simontbailey.com

888-592-1820

Sign up for our free weekly newsletter:

www.simontbailey.com

Simon's blog:

www.simontbailey.com/blog/

Follow Simon:

www.twitter.com/simontbailey

Link with Simon:

www.linkedin.com/in/simontbailey

Become a Fan of Simon:

https://www.facebook.com/SimonTBrillionaire

Book Simon to Speak at Your Event:

hello@simontbailey.com

888-592-1820